Sho   g
Hampshire Murders

Shocking
Hampshire Murders

John Barton

HALSGROVE

First published in Great Britain in 1999

British Library Cataloguing in Publication Data

A CIP record for this book is available from the British Library

ISBN 1 84114 035 X

HALSGROVE
Halsgrove House
Lower Moor Way
Tiverton EX16 6SS
Tel: 01884 243242
Fax: 01884 243325

Printed in Great Britain by MPG Ltd, Bodmin

CONTENTS

INTRODUCTION

The murders selected for inclusion in this book range in date from 1628 to 1964. Although in a sense all murders are shocking, some are undoubtedly more shocking than others. Murder by poison or strangling never seems as shocking as murder by gun or knife, which is perhaps why there are no cases of poison or strangling included here. The murders of Galley and Chater, Fanny Adams, James Parker, Mrs Chapman and Yvonne Laker are nothing if not shocking in their depravity. The murder of Fanny Adams must rank as perhaps the most gruesome of all Victorian murders, even including those by Jack the Ripper. Although some of these murders were apparently without motive, the rest exhibit a range of motives, and a varied selection of weapons with which to commit them.

The murder of Galley and Chater has been included because, even although the death of Galley may or may not have occurred in Hampshire, all the events leading up to it including the fatal blows took place in Hampshire, and it is a classic case of eighteenth-century lawbreaking.

Before 1898 an accused person was not allowed to give evidence in his or her defence. He or she could not therefore be cross-examined. This ruling applied to the first eight of the sixteen cases in this book. Most murders are not, as many people suppose, the result of violent crime, even today. Most of them occur between husband and wife, landlord and tenant, lovers, and others well acquainted with each other.

In 1970 there were 339 cases of homicide (murder and manslaughter) in England and Wales (seven cases per million people). In 1980 there were 549 cases (11 per million), in 1990 555 cases (11 per million), and in 1997 650 cases (12.5 per million), so the trend is definitely upward. Over the years 1992-97 91 per cent of male and 74 per cent of female homicide suspects were convicted (46 per cent of the males for murder and 54 per cent for manslaughter, 21 per cent of the females for murder and 79 per cent for manslaughter). Perhaps more reassuring to the public is that in 1997 90 per cent of homicides were cleared up by the police.

All but two of the accounts of these murder cases are based on the reports of the inquests, magistrates proceedings and trials in the *Hampshire Chronicle*, *Southern Evening Echo* and *Portsmouth Evening News* and I am indebted to the editors of the *Hampshire Chronicle*, *Southern Daily Echo* and *Portsmouth News* for permission to refer to those reports. The two exceptions, which occurred before there were any local newspapers, are the Duke of Buckingham and the Galley/Chater murders. I should also like to thank the staff of the Hampshire Local Studies Library for much help with documents and queries. The illustrations are reproduced by permission of the above newspapers' editors; Hampshire County Library (the picture of Frederick Baker's execution, the report of the trial of the murderers of Thomas Webb and the cover of the book about the murders of Galley and Chater); Mr and Mrs Gale (Hindhead Chase); and Mr and Mrs Franklin (Cricketers Cottage). All the other photographs were taken by the author.

THE MURDERER IS A HERO

George Villiers, 1st Duke of Buckingham, in 1628 had become the most-hated man in England, no mean achievement for a man aged only thirty-six. What had he done to deserve this unwanted reputation? He was by all accounts a charming, courteous and handsome man, so what was the reason for his unpopularity? Villiers was born in 1592, the son of a Leicestershire knight, and at the age of twenty-one was introduced to King James I. The King became infatuated with the young man, the beginning of a lifelong love and friendship. In the next few years honours were heaped on young George Villiers. In rapid succession he became a Gentleman of the Bedchamber, a knight, a viscount (1616), an earl (1617), a marquis (1618) and finally Duke of Buckingham (1623) at the age of thirty. He became the first duke for nearly a century who was not of royal blood.

George Villiers achieved a hold over King James that no royal favourite had ever previously attained, and his position as confidant and adviser was never threatened. He had simply become indispensable to the King and was treated like one of the family, indeed the equal of the future Charles I, eight years his junior. He had supplanted the Earl of Somerset in the King's affections long before the Earl's downfall. He became involved in all the affairs of state in the later years of James's reign, but his naval expeditions, the part he played in the organization of the Navy and his visits to Portsmouth are particularly relevant to this story. In October 1618 he became Lord Admiral of the Fleet jointly with the old Earl of Nottingham. When the Earl retired three months later Villiers became sole holder of the rank, and called himself Lord High Admiral. To his credit he tried to abolish the corruption in naval circles and to halt the decline in the fleet.

In James I's reign Portsmouth's decline as a port had reached its lowest point. The peace with Spain soon after the King's accession put an end to the piracy in which the ships and merchants of the town had taken part. There was little work in the dockyard and the Navy and its ships were neglected. In 1623 Henry VII's dock was filled in with rubble to prevent erosion by the sea and it was not replaced for another thirty years. The dock could have been saved but some members of the Navy Board had financial interests in Chatham dockyard and were therefore in favour of closing Portsmouth dockyard, which consisted mainly of storehouses and had no permanent body of shipwrights until 1645. But after Charles

I's accession there was a slow and steady improvement, some of it due to Buckingham's belated interest.

Portsmouth in the early seventeenth century was almost entirely enclosed by defensive works. From the sea it was protected by the Square and Round Towers and the Long Curtain, and from the land by ramparts and ditches. Entry to the town was via the Landport Gate, the Quay Gate and the Point Gate. The area now known as Point was undeveloped and the area now occupied by Southsea was marshland and common. The dockyard was separated from the town by fields and foreshore.

Buckingham in the end achieved more than could have been expected of him and the Navy Commissioners who were trying to introduce reforms were certainly glad of his support. He obtained money to improve and enlarge docks and storehouses, introduced Dutch rope-makers and set up a gunnery school. The defences of Portsmouth were now in a poor state. Southsea castle was burnt out by accident, but it had been neglected for so long that it made no difference. Buckingham became intent on improving Portsmouth dockyard and brushed aside all those whose vested interests were elsewhere, such as Sir William Burrell, who insisted that the site for a new dock was unsuitable but was the very same person who had ordered the filling-in of the old dock on the same site.

Charles and Buckingham went to Spain in 1623 in an attempt to win for the Prince the hand of the King of Spain's eldest daughter. They failed and when they arrived back in Portsmouth they received a great welcome from the local people, who were overjoyed to learn that the future King was not to have a Catholic wife. While he was in Portsmouth Buckingham was told of the sad decline of the port and of the many defects that needed to be remedied, and he appeared to lend a sympathetic ear. But his prime concern in the immediate future was to take revenge on Spain for the humiliation he and Charles had just suffered. He led England into an unsuccessful attack on Cadiz, from which few people emerged with any credit. One who did so, however, was Captain John Mason, the cousin of one of Buckingham's secretaries, whose destiny was soon to be linked with Buckingham's in an unforeseen way. At the age of twenty-four Mason had commanded an expedition to the Hebrides, and later spent six years as governor of a colony in Newfoundland. Portsmouth was not involved in the Cadiz expedition, but some of the ships returned there with their dead and dying crews. John Mason could see for himself now the consequences of an ill-prepared and disorganized fleet, for which no blame attached to him as commissary general. At this time no ship construction was being carried on at Portsmouth and there was much hardship and misery through lack of work and trade.

The next attack was on France, aimed at relieving the Protestant seaport of La Rochelle, currently besieged by the King of France. A fleet and an army had to be assembled at Portsmouth. Captain Mason had bought the best house in the town, then known as the Greyhound Inn (now Buckingham House, 11 High Street). As paymaster of this army Mason struggled to pay the men with the pitiful amounts of money that reached him from London out of the large sums that had been voted for the expedition. Officers were expected to pay their men out of their own pockets and innkeepers and householders to provide free lodgings until more money arrived. That Mason managed to provide pay and billets for the men says much for his powers of persuasion. This expedition failed as pathetically as the one to Spain, and only half the troops and seamen survived, the rest returning broken in health and spirit. Those who returned were refused lodgings by the residents because of their violent behaviour and infections, so many deserted and formed themselves into desperate and uncontrollable gangs of thieves, stealing naval stores to make up for the pay they had not received.

After the two fiascos in Spain and France the House of Commons, by now disenchanted with Buckingham, prepared a bill of impeachment against him containing 16 charges. The King averted this by dissolving Parliament, a highly unconstitutional procedure. This served only to make Buckingham even more unpopular. In 1628 Buckingham persuaded the King to send another expedition to La Rochelle, and to transport the soldiers a fleet was to be assembled at Portsmouth again.

Buckingham's support of the Huguenots did not make him popular in England, and anger was expressed in many quarters. An astrologer whom he was in the habit of consulting, Dr John Lambe, was beaten to death by a London mob simply because of his connection with the Duke. Another astrologer, Lady Eleanor Davis, insisted that the Duke would not live beyond August, but many people with no pretensions to forecasting the future would have taken a bet on that anyway.

Both James I and his son Charles I believed in the divine right of kings and considered themselves above the law, but whereas James at least in practice acted in accordance with the law Charles treated Parliament with contempt from the outset. His attempts to raise money without the authority of the Commons ended with his having to agree to a Petition of Right, which brought him a little temporary popularity. Not so Buckingham, who continued to be abused from all quarters, and as the months went by the people's anger intensified. Scarcely a week passed without a forecast of his imminent and inevitable end. On 12 August 1628 he left London with his wife, but not before making his will and calling on the Bishop of London, a sign that he was getting worried. His unpopularity was now such that he was warned to wear armour against a possible assassination, but haughtily he refused. Some premonition, however, had made him say to his wife before leaving London, 'Some adventure may kill me.' She went to Portsmouth to stay with John Mason while Buckingham rode to Southwick to stay with the King for a day or two.

Buckingham stayed with Mason at his house, surrounded by a motley crowd of army and navy officers, courtiers, tradesmen and people who had nothing else to do but be seen in his company. The Petition of Right had just become law, whereby householders were not forced to billet soldiers against their will. Mason accomplished the task of billeting the soldiers and paying them with such success that he soon had a reasonably happy body of men. It was a different matter, however, with the seamen, who had not been paid and were in a rebellious mood.

On leaving on the morning of 17 August to visit the King at Southwick, Buckingham was surrounded in his coach by a large crowd of seamen. One of them tried to pull him out of the coach at which Buckingham, who never lacked courage, leapt out and arrested him and carried him into Mason's house. After his departure, however, the seamen forced Mason to release the man by threatening to pull Mason's house down. When Buckingham returned, he summoned a council of war, which sentenced the mutinous seaman in his absence to death. He was soon recaptured and was on his way to prison when a mob of seamen attempted to rescue him. This precipitated a battle between the army officers and the rebellious seamen, ending in the latter being driven back to their ships minus two dead and several wounded. To get rid of the provocation to violence which this seaman presented Buckingham decided to hang him immediately, on the gibbet at Southsea. It went against his better nature to do this but he thought that in this case it was essential to maintain discipline. Many professional agitators were busy whipping up rebellion amongst the sailors and it seemed that Buckingham was in serious danger the longer he stayed in Portsmouth.

At about this time an army lieutenant named John Felton bought a dagger at a London cutler's shop and sewed it into his pocket lining. He set out to walk to Portsmouth as he could not afford the coach fare, and four days later, on 23 August, he arrived at the house in High Street where the Duke was staying. He entered the house without being noticed and hid behind a curtain. Buckingham had just been given the news that La Rochelle had been relieved without the necessity for an English expedition and a group of French Huguenot officers were trying to persuade him that it could not be true (it was untrue). He ordered his coach to be ready to take him to see the King and ate a hasty breakfast. He got up from the table and walked towards where Felton was hiding, then stopped to speak to Sir Thomas Fryer, one of his colonels, who had some business to discuss. Felton stepped out, leaned over Fryer's shoulder and thrust his dagger into Buckingham's chest. As the Duke staggered into the hall, wrenching the knife from the wound and crying, 'The villain has killed me,' Felton made his escape not into the street as he probably intended but into the kitchen by mistake. The Duchess, hearing the commotion, rushed downstairs to find her husband dying on the floor.

It is said that those searching for the murderer were shouting, 'A Frenchman! A Frenchman!', in the mistaken belief that one of the Huguenots in the house had killed the Duke, and that Felton misheard the word and thought that they were calling his name so stepped forward and said, 'Here I am!' It seems an unlikely story because he must have known that no-one there had ever heard of him. It is more likely that having resigned himself to being caught after doing the deed he simply gave himself up. In the confusion he could probably have escaped but instead stepped forward and admitted he was the culprit. He was almost killed on the spot but two or three officers protected him and took him off to prison. When King Charles heard the news he was heartbroken, and his grief was mixed with anger when he was told that people were dancing in the streets with joy, congratulating themselves on deliverance from the evil Duke of Buckingham and all his works. In spite of Felton's insistence that he had no accomplices, Charles was sure that Sir John Eliot, a prominent Member of Parliament, was responsible for the Duke's death, and it was not long before he contrived to imprison Eliot in the Tower of London, where he died of illness.

Felton was the youngest son of a Suffolk gentleman and a lieutenant in an infantry regiment. When asked the reason for his killing he said that he had not been paid and that a junior officer had been promoted ahead of him, but that the chief reason was to do the country a service by ridding it of Buckingham. He was interrogated several times and threatened with torture by the Earl of Dorset to reveal the names of his accomplices. He said he acted alone and that if he was tortured he would say that the Earl himself was involved. This did the trick for when the Earl consulted the judges they said that torture anyway was illegal in England, whether or not the Earl was involved. Felton was imprisoned in the Tower of London awaiting trial, and since he pleaded guilty to the murder his trial was soon over. He was executed on 29 November at Tyburn in London and his body was hung in chains on Southsea beach. It is said that the remains of the gibbet where his body hung stayed on that spot for over a century. It is shown on a print of Portsmouth published in 1765.

By the time of Felton's execution news had reached London of the fall of La Rochelle. When the ships finally reached their destination they were unable to penetrate the barricades and after a time it was found that the Huguenots had surrendered anyway so the ships simply turned round and came home.

The embalmed body of Buckingham left Portsmouth borne on the shoulders of army officers and escorted by as many of the nobility as were in the town, then a convoy of coaches took it to London. The Duke was buried in Westminster Abbey after dark by torchlight procession, because the Government feared that a daylight procession would tempt the public to express their continuing hatred of Buckingham to the distress of the King. He was laid to rest in King Henry VII's chapel, the first commoner to be so honoured. A memorial by Nicholas Stone was also placed in St Thomas's church (now the cathedral) in Portsmouth. The inscription in Latin translates as: 'Sacred to the memory of George, Duke of Buckingham, son of the illustrious George Villiers, of Brooksby, in the county of Leicester, and Mary Beaumont, Countess of Buckingham, who possessed in an eminent degree the gifts of nature and fortune, together with the favour of two most excellent Princes. His exalted abilities exceeding the expectations of all men, rendered him equal to the weight of the highest employment of the state; unequal only to the shafts of envy. While he was preparing for an attack on the enemies of his country, he fell by the impious hand of an accursed assassin, on the 23rd day of August, 1628, which caused the fatal spot to be inundated by an ocean of blood and tears. In commemoration of his many excellencies and the loss she had sustained, his inconsolable sister, Susan, Countess of Denbigh, caused this monument to be erected in the year 1631. Reader, if thou hast any yearnings of affection within thee, bewail with indignation the fate of this great man.' (Which only goes to prove that one should not believe everything that one reads on a memorial.)

Felton, a man of few words, had apparently been incited to commit his murder by delays in receiving his pay and at being overlooked for promotion. That he expected to die instantly after the deed was evident by the fact that he had stitched a piece of paper in his hat with words to the effect that a man is 'cowardly and base' who is not willing to sacrifice his life for God, his king and country, and that if God had not taken away our hearts for our sins, Buckingham would not have gone so long unpunished. As far as the law was concerned he was just a common murderer, but to the people of England he was a hero who had committed no crime. In the end he himself had a change of heart and came to believe that he had been guided by the Devil rather than by God, and regretted his deed. His body was hung in chains at Southsea and unlike Buckingham he had no splendid tomb and epitaph, but to the people of England he was the hero and Buckingham was the villain. Poems in his praise were widely circulated. It can safely be said that this was the most popular murder, perhaps the only popular murder, ever committed in England.

'THROW HIM DOWN THE WELL'

In the early and mid-eighteenth century smuggling was widespread around the coasts of Great Britain. The smugglers, who worked in gangs of as many as 60 men, were violent, desperate and well-armed, and would stop at little to get their own way. The customs officers did their best but their lives were at risk whenever they confronted a gang. The local residents were usually sympathetic to the smugglers and rarely reported them to the magistrates, who were too often unwilling or afraid to punish them anyway. Smuggling became so widespread and profitable because of the customs and excise duties imposed on a wide range of goods in order to raise revenue to pay for the long succession of wars between 1739 and 1815. There was no shortage of recruits to the smuggling business when a man could earn more in one night than in a whole week working for a farmer. So by mid-century smuggling had become socially acceptable, at least to the poorer classes who made up the majority of the population. Many honest traders were forced to buy from the smugglers in order to stay in business and when this happened of course the smugglers made even more profit. In spite of this the Government could not see that the abolition of customs duties was the answer to smuggling.

Tea was one of the chief commodities smuggled into the country because it was normally so expensive. Tea first became available to the public in about 1651 and by 1750 it had become a national drink. It cost seven shillings a pound in a shop (about a week's wages) but smuggled tea cost only two shillings a pound on the Continent, the difference accounted for by four shillings and ninepence a pound customs duty. Smuggled tea sold in London for five shillings a pound and therefore benefited the poorer classes. All tea at that time came to Europe from China, and most tea sold in Great Britain had been smuggled. The consumption of tea rose throughout the eighteenth century, as was generally observed, but official imports showed no rise and the amount of duty collected declined instead of increasing. By about 1750 4 million pounds of tea (nearly 1800 tons) were consumed annually, but only about one-fifth of this had been subject to duty. Most of the smuggled tea was brought to the south coast by sailing ships, perhaps as many as twenty or thirty landing their cargoes every week. If only one cargo in every three was saved the smugglers would make a profit, but in practice such was the ineffectualness of the customs officers that most were landed safely. Not the least part of the sorry business was that the money paid by the smugglers for their tea went to the country's enemies abroad.

The most notorious of all the gangs of smugglers in southern England was known as the Hawkhurst gang, from the village in Kent that was their headquarters. One day in September 1747 their cutter the *Three Brothers* left Guernsey with a cargo of brandy, rum and tea and set sail for the Hampshire coast. The tea weighed about 40 cwt. and cost them nearly £500, but as the duty on tea had been reduced two years ago from four shillings and ninepence to one shilling a pound it was not going to give them very much profit. They probably thought that a small profit was better than none at all. Arriving off the port of Poole in the late afternoon the *Three Brothers* was unlucky enough to be spotted by Captain Johnson aboard his private revenue cutter the *Swift*. These private cutters or privateers were licensed by the Customs and Excise to chase and seize smugglers in return for a percentage of whatever goods they confiscated. Captain Johnson was well known to smugglers as a determined man and he gave chase for some hours, gradually overhauling the *Three Brothers*. At last the smugglers decided that the game was up, so lowered a small boat and escaped while Johnson and his men examined the cargo. The captured cutter was taken to Poole quay and the tea and other goods were deposited in the custom-house.

When the smugglers arrived back at Hawkhurst they were not the most popular of men and the man in charge of the cutter, Perrin, was probably lucky not to get lynched. The gang forthwith began to plot how to recover their tea and decided that they would ride to Poole and raid the custom-house. So one night 30 of them set out from Sussex on their horses, arriving at Poole two days later in the late evening. On the way they had recruited 30 other men to act as lookouts on the roads out of Poole when they had finished their business. When they reached the town two men were sent on ahead to see whether the coast was clear. For all they knew the custom-house might have been guarded by a platoon of soldiers. One of the men rode back with equally bad news – there were no soldiers but a revenue cutter was moored right opposite the custom-house with its guns facing the quay. A furious argument then ensued; some of the smugglers wanted to call off the raid, some wanted to proceed with it. After an hour or two of indecisiveness the other man returned with good news. The falling tide had taken the cutter's guns below the level of the quay and it would not now be able to fire them across the quay.

The gang left their horses in charge of Perrin and another man while they cautiously approached the custom-house on foot. All was quiet so they forced open the main door with iron bars and the inner doors with hatchets. They carried out their two tons of tea wrapped in oilskin bags and left everything else in the store – they could not carry any of the other goods. The tea was packed into sacks on the horses' backs and the gang left Poole by the Fordingbridge road, having seen hardly a soul throughout the time they had spent in the town. On reaching Fordingbridge in the early morning they took breakfast at an inn and divided the tea among themselves so each man had an equal amount. On leaving the town they were cheered on their way by the inhabitants, who knew very well who they were and what they were about. One of the onlookers, a shoemaker named Daniel Chater, recognized one of the smugglers as John Diamond, with whom he had worked occasionally at harvest time. They exchanged a few words of greeting and Diamond continued on his way after giving Chater a bag of tea. This chance meeting on 7 October 1747 was to prove unlucky for Chater.

The authorities in London were bitterly angry at the news of the break-in at the custom-house and made their feelings known in no uncertain terms to the local customs officers. What made it worse was that nobody in authority knew who the culprits were. Although many people had seen the gang riding towards Poole and others had seen them at Fordingbridge there was not a word from the public, in spite of a proclamation offering a reward of £200 for information. People knew very well the fate of informers at the hands of smugglers and they valued their lives at more than £200. But Daniel Chater was an old man, and a foolish gossiping old man into the bargain. It was not long before everybody in Fordingbridge knew that he had received a bag of tea from the Poole break-in gang, and this priceless information eventually reached the ears of Mr Shearer, Collector of Customs at Southampton. Unknown to Chater, Diamond was already being held in custody at Chichester on suspicion of being one of the Poole gang. Some concrete evidence was needed to charge him, and Chater was the man to provide it, so Shearer decided to send Chater to Chichester to testify against him. Chater of course was reluctant to testify against his old friend, apart from the retribution he might receive as an informer. But it was made clear to him that the alternative was to face prosecution himself for receiving stolen goods, for which the penalty was transportation.

So on the morning of 14 February 1748 Daniel Chater and customs officer William Galley set out on horseback to visit Major Battine,

Justice of the Peace, at Chichester. Chater was only slightly mollified by the promise of a large monetary reward, as there was now a price of £500 on the head of each member of the break-in gang. What he did not know was that Galley was unarmed and as old and foolish as himself, although perhaps not so much of a gossip. They must have started out early for by noon they had reached Havant. On making enquiries there they were told that Major Battine was at his house at Stansted near Rowland's Castle. At Leigh they stopped at an inn for drinks and there they met George Austin and his brother, who said that they were going in the direction of Stansted and would show them the way. When they reached Rowland's Castle they again stopped for drinks at the White Hart inn. Why they stopped there is not clear – the Austins surely must have told them that they were almost at their destination. Whatever the reason it proved to be a fatal mistake.

Mrs Payne, the landlady of the White Hart, knew the Austins and asked them who the strangers were. George Austin replied that they were taking a letter to Major Battine. Mrs Payne immediately became suspicious and alarmed, because she knew that Battine was a senior customs official as well as a Justice of the Peace. This letter must be urgent, to require two men to deliver it on a Sunday. Unbeknown to Galley and Chater she was deeply involved in the smuggling trade herself, and her inn was a centre for local smugglers. If the Austins had known the purpose of their journey and the contents of the letter they would have taken Galley and Chater elsewhere. To avert further trouble Mrs Payne asked the Austins to take the two men away and put them on the wrong road so that they would never find Major Battine. The Austins refusing to do this, Mrs Payne decided that there was only one thing to do. She sent one of her sons to fetch William Jackson and as many other smugglers as he could find. While he was gone Galley and Chater decided to depart and asked for their horses. To delay them Mrs Payne said the stable-boy had locked them in the stables but that he would be back soon.

When Jackson and the other smugglers arrived Mrs Payne told them of her suspicions about the letter the two men were carrying. The smugglers said nothing for an hour or so except to ask Chater where he was going, and they all sat in the bar drinking with the Austins. Eventually Mrs Payne and Jackson decided that it would be best to get rid of George Austin (his brother was already fast asleep) so he was tactfully advised to be on his way. When he had gone Jackson took Chater aside and asked him where Diamond was. Chater replied that he was in custody and that he (Chater) was on his way to give evidence against him, an incredibly naive thing to say. Galley sensed that Jackson was trying to stop Chater from continuing his journey so went over to drag him away, at which Jackson struck Galley viciously in the face, knocking him down. Galley got up and said that as a King's Officer he would not put up with such treatment. Jackson was about to strike him again but was restrained by Mrs Payne's son, who fearing the consequences of striking a King's Officer told him not to be such a fool.

The smugglers then pretended to be conciliatory to Chater and Galley, plying them with drink and apologizing for Jackson's behaviour. They drank so much rum that after a time the two had to retire to a room with a bed where they fell fast asleep. While they slept the letter was taken from Galley's pocket and the contents read out to the others by William Carter (probably one of the few who could read). It became clear that if this letter were to reach Major Battine it would virtually sign Diamond's death warrant. What was to be done with the two men? Several ideas were discussed and discarded. The first was to throw the two into a well not far away, but this was rejected because the Austins could give evidence that they had been drinking at the inn with the gang. The second idea was to put them on a boat to France, but some objected that this was not a permanent solution as the two men would inevitably find their way back to England eventually. The third bright idea was to lock them up in some secret hideaway until the day of Diamond's trial, and then whatever punishment was inflicted on Diamond they would do likewise to the captives. If he was freed, they would be freed; if he was sentenced to death, so would they be. The decision in the end was made by those wives of the smugglers who were present. They persuaded their husbands, most of whom were by now much the worse for drink, that Chater and Galley should be hanged at some suitable place, and this seemed to meet with general drunken approval.

Galley and Chater were unceremoniously woken up by Jackson lashing them with a horsewhip, so that when they staggered into the kitchen blood was streaming from their faces. Outside the inn they were both put on one horse and their legs tied together. Before leaving one of the gang, Edmund Richards, brandished a pistol and threatened the Paynes and the other local men at the bar that he would blow their brains out if they dared to mention what had happened at the inn. The gang mounted their horses and set off, except for John Race who had no horse and was left behind. The horse with Galley and Chater strapped to it followed at the rear.

The road was as bad as most roads were in the mid-eighteenth century and the procession travelled very slowly. All the time the two men were whipped by one or other of the gang and they must by now have been in agonies of pain. At one point Galley's greatcoat was taken off in order to make his whipping more severe. Covered in blood it was carelessly left behind in the road and was found a day or two later. A mile from the White Hart they came to a place named as 'Dean' (probably the modern Finchdean). Twice the two captives fell so that their heads were under the horse and their legs on top. They became so weak that they had to be put on separate horses, and still the members of the gang continued to whip them. They threatened to throw Galley down a well, at which the poor man in his misery implored them to do so, but deciding that his punishment was not yet finished they set him upright again and whipped him on his way. After a short distance he called out, 'I'm falling,' at which Richards gave him a push so that he crashed to the ground. From this point on there is no mention of his being alive so he may have broken his neck in the fall. The smugglers seemed not to care whether he was dead or alive. By now they had passed Idsworth and had turned along a lane by the side of Lady Holt Park (now spelled Ladyholt Park), on the very boundary between Hampshire and Sussex. In which county Galley died it is now impossible to say, but there is no doubt that the ill-treatment that killed him was inflicted in Hampshire.

Soon after midnight, six hours after leaving the White Hart, they stopped at the house of a smuggling friend named Pescod and knocked on the door. His daughter went upstairs to tell her father who it was, but he sent word to them that he was too ill to receive them. Reluctantly they continued on their way and a few miles farther on arrived at the village of Rake, north-east of Petersfield on the road to London, where the landlord of the Red Lion, William Scardefield, was a friend of theirs. After a great deal of persuasion he let them in, agreed to get them some drinks and made a fire for them. While he was getting the drinks he saw a man propped up at the bar with blood all over his face and clothes, and when he went outside to the yard he saw a body on the ground. He asked Jackson what had happened, and was told that the gang had had a fight with some officers and that two of their friends had been injured. He was not allowed too near the man at the bar nor to look at the man on the ground, so Scardefield decided that discretion was the best for him.

In the early hours of the morning they asked Scardefield for a spade and forced him to accompany them as they led a horse carrying the body of Galley to a secluded spot, where they dug a shallow grave. Scardefield afterwards said, unbelievably, that he was not aware that they were burying a body. The gang returned to the Red Lion and spent the whole of the Monday there drinking, but not before taking Chater several miles farther to the home at Trotton of another smuggler, Richard Mills, where he was chained by the leg in a shed for the time being. That evening they decided to disperse to their various homes so that they would have alibis on the Tuesday morning.

On the Wednesday they reconvened at the Red Lion together with several newcomers (Thomas Stringer, John Cobby, Benjamin Tapner and John Hammond), making the number now present 14. The discussion centred not on whether to dispose of Chater, for that was unanimously agreed, but on the best method of doing so. One ingenious suggestion was that a gun should be pointed at his head and they would all pull a string attached to the trigger, so that all of them would be guilty of the murder. It was finally resolved that he would be taken to Lady Holt Park and thrown into Harris's well, the same one into which they had threatened to throw Galley. Why they did not decide to hang him and bury him there and then is a mystery. Perhaps they thought that a body at the bottom of a well would never be found. So they returned to Richard Mills's house to collect Chater and further discuss the business. While this discussion was going on one or other of the gang would visit Chater, strike him a few blows and verbally abuse him, until the poor old man was in the depths of misery.

They fetched Chater from the shed and made him kneel to say his prayers, whereupon they kicked him and Tapner slashed him across the forehead and nose with a knife. In spite of his great pain Chater asked him what had happened to Galley. 'We have done for him,' replied Tapner, 'and we will do for you.' They sat him on a horse and set out for Lady Holt Park, whipping him on his way. They neared the well at about midnight, and then the six who had buried Galley (Jackson, Carter, Richards, Steel, Little Harry and Little Sam) stood aside and said that it was the turn of the newcomers to kill Chater.

The seven who remained (Richard Mills and his two sons had made excuses for not coming) dragged Chater to the well and Tapner fastened a rope around his neck and told him to climb over the railings. With some help Chater managed to do so. He was now a pitiful sight with blood trickling from his many wounds. They pushed him into the well, but the rope being too short he came to rest half in and half out, so after a while they untied the rope from the railings and let him drop head first down the well, a distance of between 20 and 30 feet. They listened for some time and then heard a groan. They had to make sure that he was dead, so they went to a nearby cottage where they knew there was a ladder. They knocked up the tenant and asked to borrow it, making the excuse that one of their party had fallen down the well. Surprisingly, even although five of them had gone to fetch it, they could not lift it so returned to the well without it. They then threw down the well two large logs of wood and as many large stones as they could find. Not hearing any more groans they concluded probably correctly that Chater was now dead.

Having disposed of Chater and Galley there were two more pieces of evidence to get rid of – their horses, which could be identified. Should they turn them loose in a wood, or send them to France perhaps? Too risky so they decided that the only safe thing would be to slaughter them. When they got back to wherever the horses were (Rowland's Castle or Rake?) they found to their dismay that one of them (Chater's) had escaped and was nowhere to be found. They killed Galley's horse and cut it into small pieces. Unbeknown to the gang Chater's horse was eventually found and returned to its owner, who had hired it to the customs office at Southampton. Perhaps it had a name tag or was easily identifiable for it was unlikely to have found its own way back unaided. When Galley and Chater failed to return from their errand, Galley's greatcoat was found on the highway and one of the horses was returned, the authorities guessed that the two men had been killed and issued a proclamation with a reward for information leading to the arrest of the murderers.

For six months nothing happened. Then a magistrate received an anonymous letter saying where the body of Galley could be found. He sent men to the exact spot and Galley was exhumed. But still there was no evidence leading to the murderers. It was not long in coming, however, for shortly afterwards the name of one of the gang was revealed to the authorities – William Steel. When charged with the crime he decided to turn King's evidence and not only said where Chater was to be found but gave the names of all his accomplices. When John Race was apprehended he too gave King's evidence and the authorities proceeded to round up the gang one by one. The details of the events leading up to the two murders, from which an anonymous contemporary author compiled his account, must have been provided by Steel, who was present from start to finish of the whole sordid business.

Most of the members of the smuggling gang were found and thrown into various gaols to await trial. Because the Government wanted to make an example of these villains it was decided to hold a special assizes at Chichester on 16 January 1749 and on that day seven of them were brought to the court. Three judges had been appointed, Sir Michael Foster being the presiding judge. Thirty-three men had been called for jury service with Sir John Miller as the foreman. The witnesses for the prosecution included Race, Steel, George Austin and Scardefield. The first day was taken up with Judge Foster's opening address and the swearing-in of the witnesses, and the court then adjourned until the following day.

On the first indictment, for the murder of Chater, Tapner, Cobby and Hammond were named as principals and Jackson, Carter, Richard Mills and his son Richard were named as accessories to the murder. The evidence of the witnesses outlined the course of the events in all their grisly details, all of which had been witnessed by William Steel, whose evidence was obviously invaluable. The prisoners called no witnesses in their defence and each did his best to exonerate himself or to lay the blame on the others. After each one of them tried to say something in his defence Judge Foster demolished their excuses with a few choice words. Tapner, the one who had cut and whipped Chater so severely, said that he was forced into the affair by the threat of having his brains blown out. The judge pointed out that such a threat was not a legal defence of his action. Jackson said that he was not even present when Chater was killed. The judge replied that as an accessory he did not have to be present. It was sufficient that he had been involved in the murder by helping the others on the journey. Hammond said that he tried to escape but was threatened with a gun, Mills junior denied all knowledge of it, and Cobby pleaded ignorance of what they were doing! The judge impressed upon the jury the fact that an accessory was as equally guilty as a principal in the eyes of the law. The jury without even retiring brought in a verdict of 'Guilty' against all seven prisoners.

On the indictment for the murder of Galley, only Jackson and Carter were named as principals. The three men named as accessories, Richards, Little Sam and Little Harry, had not yet been apprehended. The evidence against them was reiterated by the same witnesses. Jackson and Carter again could produce no witnesses in their defence. Their defence counsel objected at one point that Galley had met his death in Hampshire so this was not the place to try the accused. The prosecuting counsel countered that by calling one of the men who had dug up Galley's body, who said that Steel had shown him the spot where Galley died, and that it was definitely in Sussex. This witness and Steel may both have been wrong, for even although the grave of Galley was in Sussex, there was no way of knowing exactly where he had died, and it may well have been in Hampshire. Once again without retiring the jury brought in a verdict of 'Guilty'.

Mr Justice Foster, addressing the prisoners, impressed upon them the seriousness of their crime (as if they were in any doubt) and the shocking nature of the treatment meted out to the unhappy victims. He pronounced sentence of death by hanging on all of them. Afterwards they were to be hung in chains as an example to others of like mind. Jackson had been ill throughout the trial and six hours later he died. (It was said that the thought of being hung in chains was too much for him.) He was by all accounts the most evil of all this sorry bunch and even his fellow prisoners gave him the worst of characters. He was one of the most notorious smugglers in the south of England, and it was said that he would steal anything from anybody, even from his friends.

The other six convicted prisoners made known their feelings to visitors while awaiting execution. Old Richard Mills had once been respected in the county of Sussex, but had taken to smuggling and had persuaded his two sons to take it up. He said he was not guilty of the two murders but readily admitted to smuggling. Young Richard Mills, a hardened criminal, said he was not present at the murder of Galley so could not be guilty, but nevertheless he approved of what the others had done. Cobby, a young and inoffensive character, who had obviously been led into crime by the others, was genuinely penitent. Tapner, a man of good education, refused to discuss his diabolical treatment of Chater and spent most of his time praying. Carter said that the murders would not have been committed had not Mrs Payne of the White Hart urged them to get rid of Chater and Galley. (She and her two sons were at that very moment in Winchester gaol awaiting trial.) Hammond, also a hardened criminal, said that it was no crime to kill informers.

When the prisoners were brought to the place of execution, a mile from Chichester on the Midhurst road, they were required to stand in a row in a large wagon standing under the gallows. When the hanging was over the bodies were taken to various places in the county to be displayed in public as was the custom of the day. In the eighteenth century many crimes were committed by smugglers against customs officers but the murders of Galley and Chater were probably the most shocking that ever came to light. Nothing quite so appalling had ever been known in the world of customs and smuggling, and when the details became known the public and the Government were shocked. It did have a salutary effect, however, on relations between smugglers and the public on the one hand, and between smugglers and customs officers on the other. The Galley and Chater murders proved to be important in the history of smuggling and marked a turning-point in the war against smuggling.

The account of the murders and the subsequent trial is based largely on a pamphlet, published a day or two after the execution, by 'A Gentleman at Chichester', entitled *The Genuine History of the Inhuman and Unparalell'd* [sic] *Murders committed on the bodies of Mr William Galley and Mr Daniel Chater*. It was completed on the day of the execution and the copy was sent to London the following day, the printer receiving it late at night and presumably starting work straight away. The author asks for errors to be excused as the work was done in a hurry.

MURDER BY SOLDIERS

At the end of the eighteenth century and the beginning of the nineteenth century there were periodic invasion scares in Great Britain. The threat of Napoleon and the French did not, however, result in large numbers of men enlisting in the regular army – conditions of pay and service were too wretched. The old English tradition of military conscription was now out of favour. Instead the aristocracy and the wealthy encouraged rivals to the regular army, namely the militia and the volunteers, under local control. The Government tried without much success to recruit men to the regular army, or to get them to transfer from the militia to the army. So a variety of armies came into existence, consisting of volunteers raised and paid by patriotic men or associations. They recruited men from the militia, and the militia in turn reduced the manpower of the regular army.

There were also fencibles – new regular regiments that also competed for recruits. They were raised for the duration of an invasion threat and restricted to defence of the country. These various institutions – volunteers, militia and fencibles – were more attractive to recruits than the regular army with its involvement in foreign battles and unhealthy climates. A fencible therefore was a soldier liable only for defensive service at home. (The name was a shortened form of 'defensible'.) The word 'fencible' was first recorded in 1795 in the *Annual Register*: 'The expenses accompanying the fencible cavalry.'

Sir Edward Leslie of Tarbert, county Kerry, Ireland, a wealthy and patriotic landowner, obtained permission in 1798 to raise a regiment of fencibles for service in England. He found no difficulty in recruiting officers, by granting them commissions on the understanding that they each recruited 15 men to serve in the regiment. Captains were paid about £160 and privates about £20 per annum. The regiment soon reached its full strength of about 480 men divided into ten companies each with three officers, three sergeants, three corporals, two drummers and 36 privates. It was named the Loyal Tarbert Regiment of Fencible Infantry.

In February 1799 the regiment set out for England by marching to Waterford to embark for Milford Haven in Wales. It was accompanied by about 400 women and an unknown number of children. There was no way then of sending money home to wives, who had therefore to travel with the soldiers or starve. From Milford Haven they marched via Carmarthen and Brecon to Gloucester, arriving there in May, when they were inspected by the Hampshire area commander, General Whitelock, apparently to ensure that there were no women masquerading as men in order to collect the bounty paid for signing on. In June they marched to Poole via Salisbury Plain, where the weather was so hot that they had to travel by night. Their stay in Poole lasted for two weeks, then they marched on via Ringwood and Lyndhurst finally reaching Botley on 30 July 1799 after a journey from Tarbert lasting six months. The Carmarthenshire militia whom they relieved then left Botley to return to Ireland.

Botley then had a population of about 600, consisting of 122 families in 98 houses. More people were employed in trades and manufacture than in agriculture. Where did the soldiers live at Botley? So many contemporary records mention a Botley barracks that there may have been some large huts specially built for the militia, but probably they lived in barns, stables and suchlike, while the officers lodged in private houses. There was a garrison of some sort at Botley throughout the eighteenth century so the building of barracks was possible. The arrival of over 1000 people would normally have caused some upheaval in the village but the new regiment simply replaced the militia who had been there for a long time. When General Whitelock reviewed the regiment in August he was astonished by the number of women and ordered all but 60 of them (six per company) to return to Ireland. So hundreds of women set out to walk to Bristol en route to Cork, each of them receiving an allowance of one shilling a day with sixpence for each child. In September the regiment received from the Tower of London 600 flintlock muskets with socket bayonets, and settled in for the winter. Discipline not being as harsh as in the regular army probably accounts for the fact that only five men deserted during that winter.

On the evening of 11 February 1800 two privates in the fencibles, John Diggon and Richard Prendergast, saw an old man coming out of a shop in Botley and followed him to the common at Curdridge (shown as Curbridge Common on early maps). For some reason they took him to be a rich farmer, whereas they should have realised that a rich farmer would have had a horse or a trap. These two soldiers had been robbing local people ever since they arrived in Botley and in so doing had given the regiment a bad name. The 'rich farmer' was in fact Thomas Webb, a poor seventy-year-old man from Swanmore. The two rogues robbed him of what little money he had, and for good measure stabbed and cut him with a bayonet, dragged him over a bank and threw him into a ditch, stamped on him and left him for dead. As at that time theft often brought a death sentence anyway, it is not surprising that the person robbed was then killed if he or she was the only witness.

Although weak from loss of blood the poor old man managed to crawl out of the ditch and stagger nearly a mile to the house of Daniel Barfoot, who immediately sent for a surgeon. The latter extracted from Webb's neck part of a bayonet 6 inches long. Meanwhile Barfoot and his son loaded their guns and went looking for the attackers. Webb was able to describe the men, and from his description suspicion fell on the fencible regiment. Soon afterwards he died of his wounds. Captain Massey of the Fencible Regiment, on hearing later that evening of the murder, possibly committed by two of his men, called the roll at the 'barracks' but found that none of his men was missing. He then enquired which men had been the last to return and was told that Diggon had only just come in from the canteen with something concealed under his coat. The shoemaker's bayonet was found to be missing and he was arrested (temporarily) together with Diggon, Prendergast and Sergeant Collopy.

At the inquest the following Monday Diggon, Prendergast and Collopy were found guilty of the murder of Thomas Webb and were committed to the next Winchester assizes. Meanwhile on 15 February the regiment was transferred to Winchester barracks, perhaps to placate the inhabitants of Botley, who had suffered at the hands of the military for a hundred years. At the trial on 10 March Collopy was acquitted, as also was Prendergast, in his case there being insufficient evidence, as the *Hampshire Chronicle* put it, 'to bring it home to him'. Diggon was found guilty and sentenced to execution and afterwards to be hung in chains. He admitted his guilt and 'begged the pardon' of Thomas Webb's widow and friends, and said that were he not about to die he would have contributed to the support of the widow. He said that he preferred instant death to a longer life under the guilt of such a crime. Diggon was hanged at Winchester on 17 March 1800 and his body was hung in chains on the common near where the murder had been committed. The position of the gibbet is shown on the Ordnance Survey map of 1810.

A memorial stone by the side of the road at Curdridge bears the inscription: 'This Stone is Erected to Perpetuate a Most Cruel Murder Committed on the Body of Thomas Webb a Poor Inhabitant of Swanmore on the 11th February 1800 by John Diggens a Private Soldier In the Talbot Fencibles Whose remains are Gibbeted on the adjoining Common'. The position of this memorial is also shown on the 1810 map so it must have been erected soon after the murder.

Note the two mistakes – Diggens for Diggon and Talbot for Tarbert.

The members of the regiment were upset by the damage to their already tarnished reputation and offered Webb's widow a half-day's pay from each of them. Prendergast was sentenced to 1000 lashes and to be drummed out of the regiment for being absent without leave on the night of the murder. On 16 March he received 600 of them and afterwards seemed 'not in the least affected'. He was discharged from the regiment on 10 April and taken to Southampton. According to one report he was taken to Winchester, where he received a subscription from sympathetic local residents, which seems highly unlikely. The Tarbert Fencible Regiment was disbanded on 24 June 1802 and another one was formed in its place by Sir Edward Leslie, but perhaps as well for the peace of mind of Botley residents it never came to Hampshire.

'I AM MURDERED AND ROBBED'

In 1818 four people lived at No. 41 Orange Street, Portsea, Portsmouth, a married couple, a single man and their landlady, a widow named Louisa Jennings. Thomas Huntingford, aged seventy-one, and Sarah his wife, aged sixty-one, occupied two rooms one above the other, and Samuel Beatley also had two rooms. The Huntingfords had lodged in this house for five years and Beatley somewhat longer, but he had known them for the last twenty years.

For the whole of this five years the Huntingfords had been known to indulge in drink, but it did not seem to have any adverse effect on their relationship. They had the usual husband and wife arguments, but on the whole seemed to be on friendly and affectionate terms with each other. Mrs Huntingford often complained of pains in the head and loss of memory, and was in the habit of going to the shops and forgetting what she wanted. She had lost an eye a few years ago because of some sort of inflammation in the head. Beatley had never seen any signs of insanity in Mrs Huntingford's character or appearance.

On the evening of 23 October Mrs Jennings had supper downstairs with the Huntingfords and at about 9 pm went to her room. Soon afterwards she heard the couple go upstairs to their room, Thomas Huntingford calling out, 'Goodnight, neighbour.' Beatley had already turned in for the night and had spoken to Mrs Huntingford before retiring, when she seemed quite normal. At about 3 am he was woken by the sound of someone noisily descending the stairs. He got up, opened his window, and looked into the yard, where he saw Mrs Huntingford walking to and fro in a state of great agitation. He put on his clothes and went to the door, to find Mrs Huntingford holding a candle. 'What's the matter?' he asked her. She was shaking so much that she dropped the candle. 'I am murdered and robbed,' she replied. Beatley looked at her incredulously, suspecting her of having taken leave of her senses. She seemed very much alive and not at all murdered. He called Mrs Jennings, who brought another candle. Mrs Huntingford kept repeating, 'What shall I do? What shall I do?' She went upstairs to her bedroom followed by Mrs Jennings.

As they entered the room Mrs Jennings saw Mr Huntingford lying in bed covered in blood. 'What is this?' she cried. Mrs Huntingford replied that two men had entered the house and murdered her hus-

band. 'You must be dreaming,' said Mrs Jennings, and ran downstairs to fetch Beatley and some other neighbours. Two of the neighbours, Mr Baker and Mrs Turnbull, went upstairs to look at the body.
Baker pulled back the bedclothes and noticed that only one person
had slept in the bed. Mrs Turnbull went in again a few minutes later
with Mrs Huntingford, who went over to a large chest containing a
money-box with a broken lid. Mrs Turnbull was asked to search the
dead man's pockets but found only one penny and one halfpenny.
Mrs Huntingford also went through the pockets and found a knife
and a key. Downstairs she told Mrs Turnbull that her husband had
been murdered by two men dressed as chimney-sweepers. Mrs
Turnbull told her to be careful what she said about murder. 'You will
be put on your oath what you say about it. Why did you not raise the
alarm?' 'Because,' said Mrs Huntingford, 'they said they would
knock my brains out. That is all I know about it, and all I shall say,
but I am innocent. Would anybody suppose I should murder my
husband?'

When Mrs Jennings saw Mrs Huntingford again downstairs she
was walking to and fro wringing her hands. Mrs Jennings asked her
why her husband was covered in blood. 'He is murdered,' she
replied. Mrs Jennings pointed out that all the doors of the house
were closed. 'Before my husband went to bed he went to the garden,'
said Mrs Huntingford. 'I suppose he forgot to shut the door.' Mrs
Jennings asked why she did not call for help. 'They threatened me,'
said Mrs Huntingford, 'that if I made a noise they would murder me.'
'Who were these men?' asked Mrs Jennings. She said there were two
men, a small man and a tall man carrying a tomahawk, and they
looked like chimney-sweepers because they were so black. When
they came into the bedroom they had asked for money. Mr
Huntingford then woke up and was struck with the tomahawk until
he was dead. Mrs Jennings said it was strange that she heard no
noise as she slept directly underneath the Huntingfords. Mrs
Huntingford replied, 'They had no shoes and made no noise.' Mrs
Jennings observed that if Mrs Huntingford had noticed that they had
no shoes, then she must have seen their faces and would recognize
them again. 'Don't ask me any more questions,' said Mrs
Huntingford. 'Don't bother me.'

While this conversation was proceeding Mr Huntingford was
being examined by Thomas Seeds, a surgeon. He had found the victim's face covered with blood, which had run on to the floor and the
bedclothes. As the blood appeared to have come from the mouth
Seeds assumed that there had been a rupture of a blood vessel in the

lungs. At this stage he did not suspect any foul play, although a handkerchief around the dead man's neck did for a moment suggest that he had been strangled. A few hours later Seeds returned to make arrangements for a coroner's inquest and examined the body again. This time he found five wounds on the forehead, one over the right eye, one close to the nose, one above the left eyebrow and two between the eyes. Four of these wounds had caused fractures. On the left temple there was a larger wound, large enough for him to insert his finger, which he considered was sufficient of itself to have caused death. These wounds appeared to have been inflicted with some sort of sharp heavy implement such as a bill-hook.

On the Sunday Mrs Turnbull told Mrs Huntingford that people suspected her of the murder. She replied that she didn't care what people suspected as long as she was innocent. As every one had condemned her she must 'pluck up her spirits' and 'stand in her own defence'. Police Constables Way and Carter then arrived to conduct a search, a whole day after the murder! On Mrs Huntingford's petticoat were found spots of blood. 'It is not blood,' she said. 'It is dirt. Even if it is blood, it must have lain on the bed.' One of her pockets was also bloodstained. 'It cannot be blood,' she said. She then tore the pocket from the garment and tried to hide it behind the sofa. At this point the constables placed her under arrest. At the inquest on the Tuesday the coroner's jury returned a verdict of wilful murder against Sarah Huntingford. It was reported that throughout the inquest she displayed 'the most callous insensibility'.

The trial was held on 5 March 1819, and lasted from 9 am to 4 pm. Beatley, Mrs Jennings and Mrs Turnbull gave evidence of the events on the evening of the murder. Beatley said that Mrs Huntingford's relations with her husband were the 'tenderest imaginable'. Mrs Jennings agreed with this, saying the couple lived 'very comfortably' together. No property was missing from their room. The gaoler at Portsmouth prison said that several bloodstained articles were taken from Mrs Huntingford the day after she was taken into custody. Several witnesses said that her clothes were bloodstained. On the iron bill-hook found in the coal-hole there were blood spots.

It was revealed that some time before the murder Mrs Huntingford had pawned some spoons and her husband's best coat, probably to obtain money for drink. When he asked her about the coat she must have become desperate, and she forced open his money-box as a last resort. It is hardly credible that a quiet and harmless woman would cold-bloodedly kill the man she has lived with for forty years on such a trivial matter, but these things do happen and nobody knows what went through her mind. Did she really think that her story of the two men would be believed? She had for many years kept a grocer's shop, and Mr Huntingford had been a shipwright in the dockyard for sixty years.

The judge in his summing up expressed his conviction 'in the most feeling and pathetic terms' that there could be no doubt whatever of the prisoner's guilt. The jury did not deliberate for very long and returned a verdict of 'Guilty'. The judge passed sentence in the usual form reserved for these occasions: 'That she be taken hence to the place from whence she came; thence, on Monday next, to be dragged on a hurdle, to a place of execution, there to be hung by the neck until she be dead, and her body be delivered over to surgeons for dissection. '

Henry Moody, in his *Notes and Essays* (1851), describes how Mrs Huntingford was conveyed on a hurdle (a kind of sledge) from Winchester gaol to the place of execution, Gallows Hill, where the road from Winchester to Andover diverges from the road to Newbury (now marked by a large roundabout). Thousands of people came from all over the county, especially from Portsmouth, to be entertained by the sight of a hanging. Their conduct was so bad, however, that the magistrates decided to hold all future executions inside the gaol.

Moody gives some interesting figures for executions in the county between 1771 and 1820. Of 190 executions, 36 were for murder, 29 for robbery, 23 for forgery, 14 for horse stealing and 11 for sheep and cattle stealing. From 1820 to 1850 there were 34 executions, eight of them for murder (only one for murder between 1838 and 1850). He concluded probably rightly that violent crimes were on the decrease. It is unlikely that fewer murderers were being apprehended since the introduction of local police forces from 1800 onwards.

'KILLED A YOUNG GIRL.
IT WAS FINE AND HOT'

Alton in 1867 was a quiet little country market town, where nothing exciting had happened since the Civil War, when Parliamentarians had fought their way into the parish church and massacred the Royalist troops sheltering there. It had been connected to London by rail since 1852, but the line from Alton to Winchester had been opened only in 1865.

Eight-year-old Fanny Adams and her young sister Elizabeth, whose father was a bricklayer, lived in Tanhouse Lane, which was then a street of small terraced houses running from Amery Street to the fields west of the town. On the afternoon of Saturday 24 August, a hot sunny day, they set off with their friend Minnie Warner to play in nearby Flood Meadow, a favourite spot with the young girls. There they met Frederick Baker, a twenty-nine-year-old Alton solicitor's clerk, dressed in his usual black coat and tall black hat. He followed the girls into the field and picked some berries for them, then gave the three girls a halfpenny each to buy sweets. He told Elizabeth and Minnie to go away and spend their money, and offered Fanny another halfpenny to go with him across the field. She took the money but then refused, so he picked her up and carried her away crying. Elizabeth and Minnie left the fields just as the church clock was striking four o'clock.

When Elizabeth and Minnie returned home at about 5 pm and were asked where Fanny was they said she had been taken away by a man. Mrs Adams became worried by this news and with a neighbour, Mrs Gardener, went to look for her and met Baker near Flood Meadow. To the question, 'What have you done with the child you took away?' he replied that he had not taken any child away. He admitted giving the children some halfpennies. Mrs Gardener asked him his name to which he replied, 'Never mind my name. You will find me at Mr Clement's office if you want me.' Mrs Gardener wanted to report him to the police but Mrs Adams' suspicions were allayed by Baker's calm manner and air of respectability. At 7 pm when Fanny had still not returned home a search was begun in the neighbourhood.

One of the searchers, James Gates, went into the hop-field near Flood Meadow. There he found a bloodstained child's dress, and a little farther on to his horror found a child's head on the ground between two hop-poles. He looked around and came across the leg and thigh of a child. Walking into Flood Meadow he found Fanny Adams's body, or what remained of it after all the internal organs had been cut out. These various pieces he handed to Charles White, who was also searching the fields, and White took them away in a bundle.

When Mrs Adams was told what had happened to Fanny she became hysterical and ran to tell her husband, who was playing cricket, but collapsed on the way. When he heard the news Mr Adams rushed home, seized a loaded gun and went to the fields in search of Baker. Had he gone to Baker's office he would have found him there and the day would probably have ended with a second murder. When he returned home the gun was taken from him by his neighbours and he was persuaded to stay at home until the morning.

Superintendent Cheyney was informed of the murder at about 8 pm that evening and went immediately to the fields, where he met Charles White with the bundle of Fanny's remains. On being told that Baker was the suspect Cheyney went to Baker's office and found him still there. He asked Baker whether he had heard of the murder. Baker replied, 'Yes, they say it's me, don't they? I am innocent and willing to go where you like.' Cheyney asked him what sort of knife he had on him, and Baker produced two from his pockets. After going off to speak to Mrs Gardener and Minnie Warner, Cheyney returned to Baker's office and arrested him on suspicion of murder. Baker again replied, 'I am innocent.' Cheyney told him that there were witnesses to prove that he had given Fanny Adams a halfpenny, to which Baker replied that that proved nothing, for he had often given local children halfpennies when out for a walk. Cheyney took him out of the back door to avoid the large crowd that had gathered in the street. At the police station bloodstains were found on his shirt-cuffs and trousers for which Baker could offer no explanation. Further questioned about one of his socks and a trouser-leg being wet he replied, 'Well, that won't hang me, will it?'

The next day a large number of people went to the fields out of curiosity, hampering the police in their search for further clues and parts of the child's body. More pieces were found, including the other leg and the eyes, which had been gouged out of the head. On the Sunday Baker was formally charged with the murder of Fanny Adams. Cheyney went to Baker's office and searched his desk, where he found a diary. The entry for the Saturday read 'Killed a young girl. It was fine and hot.' Confronted with the diary entry, Baker admitted that it was in his handwriting, and said that he had written it after seeing the women (Mrs Adams and

Mrs Gardener) but that he was drunk. (He had indeed been drinking in the morning, and it was said that when intoxicated he showed signs of insanity.)

The inquest was held on the following Tuesday at the Duke's Head, Alton. Maurice Biddle, a clerk in Baker's office, gave evidence of Baker's comings and goings on the Saturday. He had been out for a drink once or twice during the day, and Biddle went with him to the Swan in the evening. He told Biddle that he had been accused of taking away a child. He said that if the child was murdered he supposed that he would be blamed for it. (At that stage the body had not been found and nobody had said anything about murder.) He told Biddle that he was going away on the Monday. The boot-boy of the inn said that he was also going away on the Monday and Baker replied that they might as well go together. The boot-boy said that would not do 'because unlike Baker he could put his hand to anything'. Baker replied, 'I could turn butcher.' (Unconscious or deliberate humour?) Back at the office a short time later they heard that the child had been murdered and that Baker was suspected. 'Never, Maurice, it's a bad job for me, then,' said Baker. When the inquest jury returned a verdict of wilful murder Baker showed no sign of emotion. A large crowd surrounded the inn and two hours elapsed before it was thought safe to smuggle the prisoner out by the back door and run quickly to the police station.

On the Wednesday the remains of Fanny Adams were buried in Alton cemetery, and a large crowd attended the funeral of the town's first murder victim that most of them could remember. On the Thursday Baker was examined in front of the local magistrates in Alton town hall and was committed for trial at the next Winchester assizes. A hostile crowd had gathered outside the building and the police had difficulty in protecting Baker from the mob, who wanted to lynch him. The court was full to capacity with many people unable to gain admission. Baker seemed quite surprised and alarmed at the animosity of the crowd. He repeated that he was not guilty. 'I am as innocent as on the day I was born.'

Mr and Mrs Adams again gave evidence but they were obviously in no fit state to do so. George Adams during his evidence could not stand still but walked up and down, clasping his hands together and wiping the tears from his eyes. At one point he turned to Baker and said, 'You are a villain, indeed!' Baker affected not to hear this remark. Harriet Adams seemed to be completely overcome with grief, and could hardly bring herself to identify the clothing of her daughter.

It may not have been the first murder in Alton but it was to prove the most famous and the most shocking. When they reported the murder the national newspapers emphasized its barbarity and its apparent lack of motive. They said that it would rank with the murders by Burke and Hare and that it was the work of a lunatic because a sane man could not have done it. The *Globe* thought that such a crime was a strong argument for capital punishment. The *Daily Telegraph* said that a more horrible crime had never been committed and that the murderer was a monster who should be 'put out of the way'. There is no doubt that the country was appalled by the story. All the newspapers said that the murderer must have been insane. Had he been charged with the murder today it is indeed likely that he would have been found guilty but insane.

In October further evidence came to light. Soon after the murder became known a little boy had told his mother that at about 2 pm on the Saturday he had seen Baker leave the hop-garden and wash his hands in the stream. Seeing the boy watching him, Baker had told him to go away and repeated the order when the boy did not go. Baker had then walked away in the direction of the turnpike road (where he was seen by the toll-keeper). But the boy did not see Baker again until he was taken to an identity parade at the prison and there he failed to pick out Baker until he was nudged by his mother, who had never seen Baker before! For some unknown reason his mother told nobody of what the boy had seen until she mentioned it one day in a public house. On hearing the boy's story the police searched the stream at the spot indicated by the boy but found nothing. The boy's story revived interest in the murder, which by October had died down.

During his stay in Winchester prison awaiting trial Baker was said to be very talkative. He frequently referred to the murder, saying that his conscience was clear and wondering who the murderer could be.

The trial was held on 5 December 1867 at Winchester. The court was full to overflowing and those who could not gain admission made so much noise that the judge, Mr Justice Mellor, threatened them with imprisonment if they did not keep quiet. This had the desired effect and the trial proceeded peacefully. Mr Montague Bere, Recorder of Southampton, conducted the case for the prosecution and Mr Carter for the defence. Baker pleaded 'Not Guilty'.

In his opening remarks Bere asked the jury to forget all that they had read about the murder in the newspapers (and few murders in England had ever received such widespread publicity) and concentrate on the evidence that would be presented at the trial. He went on to describe in great detail all the circumstances of the murder and the events after the body had been found. He stressed that the evidence was circumstantial, but he hoped to prove that it formed a chain from which the accused could not escape. As for the motive behind the crime, Bere said that there could be little doubt as to the purpose for taking the child away but left the jury to surmise what he was suggesting. For the rest of the day and into the next morning witnesses for the prosecution were called and their evidence followed the same pattern as had been given at the inquest and in front of the magistrates in August.

Professor Taylor of Guy's Hospital reported the results of the examination of Baker's knives and clothes. He had found blood on most of his clothes but only in isolated spots – there was much less blood than he would have expected, in fact no more than would have been caused by a nose-bleed. The bloodstains appeared to be recent but it was impossible to say what blood it was, other than that it was the blood of a mammal. One of the knives had a small quantity of dried blood on it. As no other knife was found at the scene of the crime it was assumed that Baker had used one of his two small pocket-knives. Dr Leslie of Alton then described the dismemberment of the body in great detail, starting with the head and finishing with the internal organs. By the time he had finished his evidence most members of the jury probably wished they were somewhere else.

Carter, the defence counsel, must have realised that he had a rather hopeless task. He said that he would rely firstly on a criticism of the evidence so far heard and secondly on the state of mind of the accused, showing that he could not be held responsible for his acts. He said that if he could persuade the jury of the doubtfulness of the evidence he would not need to press the case for insanity.

He asked whether there was any motive, malice or premeditation and said that there was none. He asked why the girl had been cut into pieces and not buried, which would have served to conceal the crime more effectively, and suggested that sane people did not commit such extraordinary crimes without some motive. Carter tried to explain the diary entry by suggesting that a guilty person would not have left such incriminating evidence. (Did the entry mean 'I killed a young girl' or 'Somebody killed a young girl'?) He emphasized the insanity in Baker's family and the defects in Baker's character. He said that Baker had once attempted suicide after a love affair, and his landlady had said that he was always depressed and 'appeared wild'.

Carter called as witnesses Baker's father and sister and their family doctor, who testified to his unstable temperament. Baker's father said that after his son had suffered an attack of typhus at the age of sixteen he was always complaining of pains in his head and often burst out crying. After the failed love affair Baker had become very unsettled and decided to go into lodgings. From then on his father became worried that his son would carry out his threat to commit suicide. Baker was a member of two literary societies in Guildford and had been a Sunday-school teacher for ten years. Dr Taylor, the family doctor, said that Baker had always been somewhat weak-minded and after he left Guildford he noticed a change in his character, from being a weak and inoffensive person to 'something swaggering'.

After a review of the evidence by Mr Bere, the judge summarized the case for the jury. He said that this was one of the most remarkable cases he had ever tried. It depended largely on evidence arising from the conduct of the accused and from an entry in his diary. He complimented Carter on the skill with which he had conducted the defence and thrown doubt on some of the prosecution's evidence. He warned the jury that if they concluded that the accused was guilty of the crime but was not responsible for his acts then they must return a verdict of 'Not guilty on the grounds of insanity', but they must be very clear in their minds that that was the case.

The judge's summing-up lasted two hours but the jury were out for only fifteen minutes. When the foreman announced their verdict of 'Guilty', Baker nervously rubbed his hands together and when asked whether he had anything to say made no reply. The judge addressed him solemnly and at some length. 'You have been convicted of a crime rarely paralleled in the history of this country. For some purpose... you brutally murdered her   and dismembered her bod... it is a shock to our common humanity... You must shortly appear before the searcher of all hearts... Consider the coming judgment, and the interests of your immortal soul... Prepare for your dread account (The judge liked that phrase – he said it twice.)...hanged by the neck until you be dead... may God have compassion on your soul.' This funereal speech visibly affected many of the people in court, but not the prisoner, who walked calmly away from the dock.

Baker's execution at Winchester prison at 8 am on Christmas Eve 1867, witnessed by more than 5000 people, was one of the last to be held in public in England. (The last was on 26 May 1868 at Newgate in London.) The *Hampshire Chronicle* reported that a large proportion of the crowd were women, and that there were hundreds of working-class people from Winchester, Southampton and Portsmouth, a few shopkeepers and a small number of 'nondescripts'. The huge crowd watched in silence as Baker was led to the scaffold, the last prayer was said and the bolt withdrawn from under him.

In a letter to Fanny's parents, made public after his execution, Baker expressed his deep sorrow and asked for their forgiveness. He wrote that 'in an unguarded hour and not with malice aforethought, but being enraged with her crying' he killed Fanny 'without pain or struggle'. Mr and Mrs Adams said that they were willing to forgive Baker and expressed their satisfaction with his confession.

Baker's decision to cut Fanny into small pieces seemed inexplicable for his only hope of concealing the crime would have been to bury the body. It was suggested at the trial that he did so in order to conceal the fact that he had violated her, but in his letter to her parents he denied the accusation (and the medical evidence corroborated his statement). He had returned to his office in mid-afternoon (to get a knife?), then paid a second visit to the fields when he met Mrs Adams and Mrs Gardener. Did he cut up the body on this second visit? If not, what was the purpose of it?

The murder of Fanny Adams will always be remembered as one of the most horrible in the annals of crime, not only for its gruesome character but also for its apparent lack of motive. Soon after the murder sailors in the Royal Navy were issued with tinned meat of a quality even more inferior than usual. With the macabre humour of the lower deck they named this meat 'Sweet Fanny Adams'. The name was included in a slang dictionary of 1889 with the meaning 'tinned mutton'. The name stuck but over the years it acquired a different meaning, that of 'nothing' or 'worthless'. A sad memorial for a tragic tale.

THE MURDER OF JAMES PARKER

In the early afternoon of Friday 9 April 1886 Henry Piper walked into the field at the bottom of what was known locally as Barton Hill, between Winchester and Kings Worthy. Henry, a farm labourer employed by a local farmer, was looking for a drill that he had been told was in this particular field. He soon found the drill but could not see the shafts anywhere so he went over to a hayrick and kicked a large pile of loose straw thinking that they were underneath it. Under the straw he found not the shafts but a body – the body of a young man with terrible injuries to his head and his throat cut from ear to ear. Henry's usually uneventful life had not conditioned him to shocks such as this but gathering his wits he hastened away to call the police.

Because the constable at Kings Worthy was ill, Police Constable Gladwell was summoned from Easton. Near the body he found the top of a razor case but nothing that could have inflicted these ghastly injuries. He borrowed a farm-cart and took the body to the Cart and Horses inn at Kings Worthy, where he searched the pockets of the dead man's clothes, which were very wet. In one pocket he found a piece of sodden paper on which were written words to the effect that James (the surname was not given) joined a ship in London on 26 March and was discharged at Southampton on 6 April. Meanwhile a message had been sent to Superintendent Sillence at Winchester, who on hearing that the dead man reported earlier had apparently been murdered, hurried over to Kings Worthy with Detective-Inspector Lawler to inspect the body and to gather details of the crime. He read with great interest the scribbled note found in one of the dead man's pockets.

At 5 am the following morning Sillence set out for Southampton docks with Lawler. In 1886 the docks were a hive of activity, even at the early hour of 6 am. Six years later they were taken over by the London and South-Western Railway Company, and trade increased threefold by the First World War. Sillence knew his way around the docks and made straight for Chapel Quay. There he learned that a vessel corresponding to the one he wanted had left the previous day for Eling, a mile or two up-river, and that two men, one of whom fitted the description of the dead man, had been discharged from the ship before it sailed.

Sillence and Lawler took a train to Totton and walked to the quay at Eling. There they were told that the vessel they wanted had moved on to Redbridge. Eventually they found Captain Frank Roberts, the master of the ketch *Nellie*, who recognized the piece of paper found on the victim and confirmed that it was in his handwriting. It had been given to one of the two men who had been paid off at Southampton on Wednesday 7 April. (He had evidently written the wrong date on the note.) Roberts said that he had engaged the two men in London, one at Millwall and one at Greenwich, but that he did not know their surnames. Sillence was disappointed at this – without knowing either name he would not get very far with his enquiries. He asked to talk to the rest of the ship's crew and to his delight elicited some valuable information. One man remembered that the younger of the two had addressed the other as 'Brown', and that Brown had said that his Christian names were the same as those of the Prince of Wales – 'Albert Edward'. Brown had also mentioned that at Greenwich he had been a licensed waterman and that his father, also a waterman, was nicknamed 'Boxer'.

Lawler was immediately sent to London on the 11 am train from Totton, while Sillence went to Southampton station to make enquiries. There he learned that on Wednesday last a young man named James Parker had forwarded a seaman's bag to Nine Elms station in London, presumably to be collected or forwarded to his home in Clapham. He then sent a telegram to Chief Inspector Williamson at Scotland Yard with details of the crime and a request to find 'Boxer' Brown and his son. When Lawler arrived at Greenwich police station he found that Albert Edward Brown had already been arrested by the CID, the information sent by Sillence regarding 'Boxer' Brown having been sufficient to locate this particular Brown among all the many Browns living in Greenwich. Lawler brought Brown back to Winchester on the train arriving at 9.30 pm Saturday evening, just 28 hours after Gladwell first saw the body and 16 hours or so after Sillence and Lawler had set out for Southampton. Sherlock Holmes himself could not have done much better than Superintendent Sillence.

Brown was twenty-three years old and had been married only a few months. He was arrested at his father-in-law's house, where he had arrived on Thursday evening. He protested that he was innocent of the charge. He was said to be only 5 feet 2 inches tall and his features were 'unprepossessing' – a low receding forehead and snub nose, with a moustache and hair on his chin.

Sillence followed Lawler to London and on the Sunday went to

Clapham, where he managed to locate the relatives of young James Parker. His father had been a coachman but was now unemployed. By means of part-time jobs his wife and daughter kept the family from starving. Young James had never been away from home before this fateful trip; dire necessity had forced him to take a job on board ship. To Sillence fell the painful task of breaking the news of the murder of their only son.

Mr Parker returned to Winchester with Sillence in order to identify the body of his son. The funeral took place on the Tuesday at Kings Worthy church, when about 150 people attended. Why such a large number came to the funeral of a stranger raises an interesting question – was it out of sympathy or curiosity? Indeed the vicar went so far as to say to them that they were there not on a sightseeing occasion but at a burial service.

The inquest was held on the Monday, the day before the funeral, at the Cart and Horses inn. The coroner, in his address to the jury, said that it was time the law was changed to avoid the necessity of having two courts that heard all the same evidence, first at the inquest and then at the trial, but until such time as the law was changed they must do their duty here today. After the coroner had spoken the jury inspected the body – not a sight for the faint-hearted.

Several witnesses were called to identify Brown. They had all attended an identity parade at the prison in order to pick him out from other prisoners. Captain Roberts of the *Nellie* was asked about relations between the two men on the voyage from London. He said that they appeared to be very friendly, almost affectionate to one another, and that Brown did much of Parker's work for him when the young man became sick. Asked about Brown's possessions when leaving the ship, he replied that Brown took with him a hammer, chisel, mallet, knife and razor.

Emily Mitchell of the Hyde Tavern, Hyde Street, said that the two men had called at her public house for a drink on the Wednesday evening. They had said that they intended to walk to Basingstoke and then on to London. They were in the house about fifteen minutes and had a pint of 'fourpenny' (beer). Edward Norris, who lived at the old turnpike cottage in Worthy Road, saw the two men at about 7 pm, near the milestone in Mr Simonds's wall, walking towards Kings Worthy. They had asked him whether they were on the road to London.

Charles Bartlett, foreman at Winchester railway station, said that he had seen the prisoner on the platform at about 5.45 am on the Thursday. He could not say whether Brown had boarded a train – in any case the first one to London was not until 7.23 am. He described Brown as a 'suspicious-looking card who turned his back on him'.

Dr Richards had conducted the post-mortem examination. He stated that at least two of the blows to the head could not have been self-inflicted and that the throat must have been cut from behind and above the deceased. He went on to describe the injuries in all their gory details, but after having seen the body the jury were now probably not so shocked as they might otherwise have been.

Charles Delatouche, Brown's father-in-law, described the prisoner's arrival at his house on the Thursday evening. Brown was wearing a nearly new oilskin and said that he had bought it for 2 shillings. (It was Parker's.) Delatouche identified the top of the razor case as being the one he had given Brown two months previously. (He obviously had no intention of shielding Brown from the implications of this damning piece of evidence.) The following day Brown had remarked that he supposed Parker would be well on his way home by now.

Sergeant Morgan of the CID described Brown's reaction when charged with the murder of Parker. He had said, 'Me! I know nothing about it. I left him in Winchester.' Brown had said that on coming out of the Hyde Tavern they met a man and woman who offered to accompany them part of the way to London. He then said goodbye to Parker because he wanted to take the train. (Yet they had been seen by Edward Norris walking to Kings Worthy – the milestone is half a mile from the Hyde Tavern.)

Yet more witnesses were produced. A porter at the station had spoken to Brown just before he boarded the London train. He said the prisoner had a rough and dirty appearance and was carrying a canvas bag. Benjamin Smith and Richard Mott said that they had seen a man resembling Brown on the Thursday morning while they were on their way to Micheldever. He had come out of the field at the foot of Barton Hill at about 4.45 am. (They said it was daylight – if so it must have been later than that because sunrise on 8 April was not until about 5.30 am.)

Brown was also seen on Worthy Road by Frank Shergold, another carman, between 5 and 5.20 am. None of these carmen could positively identify the prisoner (not surprising as it must have been still fairly dark). Joseph Glasspool, a milkman, was sure that it was the prisoner he saw at about 5.10 am on Worthy Road. Brown appeared to be brushing a coat or oilskin and he asked Glasspool the way to the station. (It was not yet sunrise but it may have been light enough for Glasspool to remember Brown.) At this point in the proceedings

Brown put several questions to Glasspool regarding the exact spot where they had met. He seemed to be familiar with this stretch of Worthy Road, yet according to his previous statement he had left Parker in Hyde Street.

The coroner's jury of 15 deliberated for about forty minutes and then gave their verdict that James Parker had been wilfully murdered by Brown. The coroner agreed with their decision and said that on the evidence Brown should be sent for trial at the next assizes.

The trial was held at the Winchester assizes on Monday 10 May, Mr Justice Day presiding. The court was full to capacity and many people were unable to gain admission. Charles Mathews, the prosecuting counsel, opened the case. He stressed that the evidence to be presented was circumstantial but that it was convincing evidence none the less. He related at great length all the details of the events of that Wednesday, Thursday and Friday. He stressed the apparent good relations between the two men, and that they had agreed to walk all the way to London and had mentioned this to one or more people. By all accounts Brown had left the ship with 15 shillings and 6 pence and Parker with 6 shillings, so the story they told Mrs Mitchell at the Hyde Tavern about being penniless was obviously untrue. (Brown subsequently bought a rail ticket for 3 shillings and 6 pence and handed his wife 10 shillings.) They were later seen on Worthy Road at about 7 pm by Edward Norris, and by Jonathan Bedford, who was driving in a trap towards Winchester, a little farther on. (Sunset on 7 April was at about 6.45 pm so the light could not have been very good, and it was raining.)

Mathews made much of Brown's statement that he had left Parker in the company of two strangers outside the tavern. If it was true, why did Brown not catch a train to London that very evening – there would have been one or more? If it was true, how was it they were seen walking along Worthy Road by several witnesses? If however it was false why did the prisoner say that? Because, said Mathews, he knew he had been seen then and again the following morning. Brown had failed to explain why his often expressed resolution to walk to London was suddenly abandoned. This, said Mathews, 'was an important moment, when a guilty person is overtaken with the consciousness of his own peril.'

After the prosecuting counsel's address, all the witnesses for the prosecution were called and repeated the evidence they had given at the inquest. Mr Lopes, the defence counsel, did not call any witnesses. Mathews then gave his final address to the jury. He said that the circumstantial evidence pointed very strongly to the guilt of the prisoner. In particular he cited the razor case found near the victim and which was unquestionably the property of Brown. How else could it have got there? Where were the two persons supposedly accompanying Parker to London – were they figments of Brown's imagination? They had not come forward since the case was made known. Did they exist?

Mathews referred to witness Glasspool the milkman. Was it not strange that the accused had interrogated him as to the exact spot where they had met, in doing so more or less admitting that he was indeed the man encountered by Glasspool? Referring to the razor, knife and hammer that Brown carried in his bag from Southampton but did not have with him on arriving at Greenwich, Mathews asked whether an innocent man would dispose of his tools en route for no good reason. (Evidence had been given at the inquest that every inch of the railway track between Winchester and Woking had been searched for the murder weapons – surely an exaggeration.)

Lopes then addressed the jury. He had a difficult task. He began by stressing that all the evidence was circumstantial. It was a curious fact, he said, that there was an absence of malice, although he recognized that it was not necessary to prove malice in a charge of murder. There was also an absence of motive. Were they to conclude that Brown murdered this boy for the sake of the few shillings that he might have had? He submitted that the only reliable witness on the Thursday morning was Glasspool, and he seemed a bit too eager to incriminate the accused. Furthermore, was it the action of a guilty man to come out of the field in full view of any passers-by and go to catch a train, where he would certainly be seen by several people? Surely a guilty man would have walked away towards London?

Judge Day in his summing up said that the fact that Brown was the last person seen in the company of Parker was insufficient to prove his guilt. (Many innocent people would be convicted if that was sufficient reason.) Nevertheless the evidence of the witnesses who saw him coming out of the field, walking along Worthy Road and at the station could not be ignored. The two men were seen near the field at 7 pm the previous evening and Brown was seen near the same place at 5 am. What possible construction could be placed upon those facts but that they had both spent the night in the field? He also wondered why Brown had not taken a train on the Wednesday evening if he had decided not to walk any farther.

Brown had asserted at one stage that he had left Parker in the company of two tramps (presumably not the man and woman previously referred to). Why had he failed to give a description of the tramps when surely it would have helped his case? Nor had he told the police where he did sleep that night if it was not in the field. The judge pointed out to the jury that direct evidence was not necessarily better than circumstantial evidence, and he was always sorry when doubt was cast upon the latter. When the law spoke of doubt it meant doubt raised by the facts of the case, not doubt raised in one's mind. If there was any reasonable doubt they must acquit the prisoner, but if the facts left no reasonable doubt that the deceased met his death at the hands of the prisoner, there would be no alternative to finding the prisoner guilty. He said that it was idle to look for motive – who could possibly have any motive against a young man in a strange part of the country?

The jury retired for two and a half hours and on returning the foreman gave their verdict – Brown was guilty. The prisoner was asked whether he had anything to say. He nervously rubbed his hands together and replied, 'Yes, I can prove there are some false witnesses here,and I can prove that.'

The judge then pronounced sentence of death by hanging, at which Brown again muttered something about false witnesses. The fact that the jury took such a long time to come to a decision might seem surprising, but there must have remained an element of doubt in a reasonable person's mind. Brown might not after all have committed the murder. He could have woken up in the field, decided to catch a train and said goodbye to Parker, and some person or persons unknown (such as the tramps) could have gone into the field and murdered the young man while he was dozing. That would have fitted the facts of the case nicely and explained Brown's casual demeanour after leaving the field and on arriving at his home.

All doubts, however, were dispelled when a few days after the trial Brown made a full confession. The text of this was not circulated to the press because prison regulations did not allow it, but it seems that Brown said he had no intention of murdering Parker when he first attacked him and that his sole motive was robbery. At the same time he told the police where the murder weapons were to be found and sure enough the hammer was found in a hedge at the top of Barton Hill some 200 yards from the scene of the murder and not far away was the razor.

This was one of the most horrific and notorious murders of the late nineteenth century. If it had not been for the quick action and deductive powers of Superintendent Sillence, however, it is likely that the culprit would never have been traced. On trivial pieces of evidence such as the scribbled note by Captain Roberts many a case has been brought to a successful conclusion. If Brown had only thought to search Parker's pockets and destroy that note he might never have been found out.

The headstone erected over Parker's grave reads:

This stone was erected by sympathising friends
JAMES STANDLEY PARKER.
April 8th, 1886
Aged 18 years.
Enter not into judgment with Thy servant; for in
Thy sight shall no man living be justified.
For the enemy hath smitten my life down to the ground.
Ps. cxliii., 2.3.

Many contributions towards its cost were received from local people. The maximum accepted from any one person was a shilling, and from a poor person a penny. The headstone now lies flat on the ground, its lettering very worn, on the south side of Kings Worthy churchyard. Perhaps one day it will be re-erected as a mark of respect for this unfortunate young man.

'YOU SHALL NOT THROW
ANY MORE TEA AT ME'

Cricketers Cottage at Blacknest, in the parish of Binsted near Alton, is situated about 75 yards off the road from Bentley to Bordon, not far from the Jolly Farmer, which stands at a crossroads to the south on the edge of Alice Holt Forest. In 1894 it was a public house named the Cricketers Inn. The road was not very busy then. (The first motor car on British roads appeared in November that year.) There was, however, enough local custom to support the inn and it probably attracted a reasonable trade. Bentley railway station was just over a mile away. In theory the landlord was ninety-three-year-old George Chappell, but he was infirm and the inn was run by his daughter Mrs Frances Knight, aged fifty-three, and her husband Cyrus Knight, aged forty-five. They had been married for seven years and were both well known in the neighbourhood. Cyrus Knight was a hire carter by trade and no doubt the couple needed the extra income from his work. With them lived Mrs Knight's adopted son, fifteen-year-old William Brewer, who had been with her nearly all his life.

On the evening of Friday 28 September William Brewer arrived home at about 7.30 pm. What happened next was described by him at the inquest held the following week. He said that he sat down to his tea in the kitchen and Mrs Knight fetched her husband from the tap-room. Knight had been drinking but was not drunk and when he had finished a game of dominoes he came for his tea. When he sat down Mrs Knight started to scold him for stopping and drinking at public houses, to which outburst he made no reply. Knight then poured the contents of the milk jug into his cup of tea, so Mrs Knight took his cup and poured some of the milk into her cup and some into Brewer's cup. Without saying a word Knight then threw what remained in his cup over the front of his wife's dress. In retaliation she threw the contents of her cup over Knight, and he then threw his cup at her which after hitting her smashed on the floor.

At this point Knight stood up and said something to the effect that she would not throw any more tea at him. He collected his jacket from the passage and went into a small room adjoining the kitchen. After a few minutes he reappeared with a shot-gun and walked across the kitchen to the door leading to the garden and apparently went out. Two or three minutes later Brewer saw the muzzle of the gun protruding inside the half-open door and pointing at Mrs Knight; he could not see who was holding the gun (it was by then dark outside). Before he could shout to Mrs Knight, who was washing up the crockery, the gun was discharged twice and she fell to the ground with blood pouring from a wound in her neck.

Brewer screamed and ran into the tap-room, where three or four men were drinking and playing dominoes. Jim Sampson Light, a gypsy dealer and friend of Knight, rushed into the kitchen with Brewer and looked at Mrs Knight, who was by now quite dead. They both ran out of the house to call for help and to send for the police. Meanwhile Knight himself had disappeared but had left his gun leaning against the rear wall of the building. William Kay, a surgeon, came to the inn at about 10 pm and examined the body. He concluded that Mrs Knight had died almost instantaneously from a bullet wound below the left jaw.

Early next morning Inspector Hawkins of the Alton police arrived at the Cricketers Inn and examined the dead woman and searched the kitchen. At about 8 am Cyrus Knight appeared at the back of the inn and Hawkins, on being told who he was, arrested him on suspicion of murdering his wife. Knight replied, 'I could not help it. The gun went off as I went out of the door.' He asked to see his wife and Hawkins allowed him to look at the body for half a minute. Knight was very quiet as he did so but did not seem unduly affected.

The inquest was held on the following Tuesday in one of the bedrooms at the Cricketers Inn, scene of the tragedy. Knight was present at his own request. All the members of the jury knew him and some were his friends. A crowd of people stood outside in the road waiting for the verdict. Knight was a tall, strong, well-built man who walked with a limp and he was wearing the rough working clothes in which he was arrested. He listened carefully to the evidence of the witnesses. The coroner asked him whether he wanted any paper to make notes and Knight replied that he was unable to write.

The first witness was William Brewer. He was closely questioned on the subject of previous quarrels between the Knights, and after much hesitation on the boy's part the coroner managed to extract from him the information that the couple had quarrelled only when Knight had had too much to drink and that he had once threatened to 'do for the old b—'. Brewer understandably was in a delicate position, not wanting to tell lies yet probably wanting to shield his stepfather if possible. Brewer was then asked questions about the events from the time he arrived home until the shots were fired. He explained all the details of the tea-throwing episode and of how Knight then went to the next room and came back with his gun. Asked about the muzzle of the gun peeping through the door he said it appeared to be aimed at Mrs Knight but that he was unable to see who was holding it because the door screened whoever it was.

Sampson Light said that the gun in court was the one he had given Knight to sell for him two months previously but that so far it had not found a buyer. Asked about Knight's condition on the evening in question, Light replied that he was 'not sober but not drunk – about half-drunk'. As to relations between the Knights that evening he said that they seemed to be on good terms. Harriet Collins lived in a cottage next door to the Knights. (It was part of the same building.) She described how she heard two shots and then the screams of the boy Brewer. She said that the couple sometimes quarrelled after Knight had been drinking and that he had threatened Mrs Knight more than once, saying that he would kill her. She went on to say that Knight was very quiet when sober but when drunk was malicious. She had more than once had to wipe the blood from Mrs Knight after Knight had struck her. William Kay, the surgeon, said that the victim died from the laceration of all the blood vessels in the neck, causing a haemorrhage. A post-mortem revealed that the wound in the neck was the sole cause of her death.

Knight was sworn in as a witness and gave his version of the events. He said that the gun had been loaded three days previously and he was going to take it outside to 'shoot it off'. He held the gun in his right hand in an upright position and when going out of the door was forced to 'chuck' the gun on to his left arm in order to close the door, and the gun went off accidentally. He said that he was 'not looking in the door at all'. 'I heard my missus say she was shot, and I stood the gun down and away I went – I don't know where I went to.'

The coroner reminded the jury that all they had to do was to say whether or not a prima-facie case of murder had been made out. There were two alternatives to consider; that Knight wilfully and deliberately shot his wife or that it was an accident. Brewer was obviously doing his best to screen his stepfather but his evidence was crucial to the case. The boy had not actually seen who had fired the shots but it must have been Knight, a fact substantiated by his statement that the gun went off accidentally. The coroner said that drink was no excuse for crime and a drunken man was as liable for his actions as a sober man. The jury were unanimous in finding Knight guilty. The crowd outside the inn showed no anger towards him when he came out, in marked contrast to the attitude towards Frederick Baker at Alton in 1867.

At the magisterial proceedings on the Thursday much of the previous evidence was presented again, with one or two additions. All the witnesses said that there was a marked change in Knight's demeanour after he had been drinking and that there were very often quarrels when he was drunk. Mrs Collins elaborated on her previous statements and said that she had often seen Knight hitting his wife and that more than once 'she has been all but dead'. Brewer described relations between the two as 'uncomfortable'. Knight was committed to stand trial for murder at the next Winchester assizes.

The trial began on Friday 16 November with Sir William Grantham presiding. In his opening address the judge said that he was sorry to see that the list of cases on this occasion was so large, with three cases of murder. He exonerated the city of Winchester from blame for the extra crimes, which had occurred in other parts of the county where there was a larger population of a 'rougher kind'.

The prosecuting counsel, Mr Blake Odgers, called the witnesses who had previously given evidence. Brewer when called now said that Mr and Mrs Knight lived 'unhappily', that Knight had struck her, and had threatened he would 'do for the old b—'. Odgers referred Brewer to the evidence he had given at the inquest and said that did not correspond with the evidence he was now giving. He read out from the *Hampshire Chronicle* the full extract of the inquest proceedings. Brewer replied that what he had said at the inquest was correct.

Mr Smith, an Alton gunsmith, said that the gun had rebounding locks and the triggers were bound to be at half-cock. He had tested the gun and found that it was impossible to fire it at half-cock. It had to be at full-cock and therefore in his opinion it could not be discharged accidentally. Mr Bullen, the defence counsel, referred to Knight's statement that his wife had exclaimed, 'I'm shot.' Dr Kay the surgeon, when recalled by the judge, said that it would have been impossible for the woman to have spoken because of the severity of the wound. Odgers, in his summing up for the prosecution, said that the jury must surely be convinced from the evidence that Knight had deliberately killed his wife.

Mr Bullen, summing up for the defence, said that his only evidence would be the character of the accused, because Knight himself could offer no evidence, and the only living witness (Brewer) had been called by the prosecution. He admitted that he had a difficult task, and in the end it would be up to the jury to decide whether

Knight should live or die. He would not appeal to their sympathy but to their sense of justice, and he would ask them whether they were satisfied that the evidence was sufficient to condemn the prisoner to the gallows. He pointed out that Knight had a good character and a 'kindly disposition' and would therefore be unlikely to commit such a cold-blooded crime.

Bullen said that his defence would not be one of manslaughter but would rest on Knight's plea of an accident. He thought the prosecution were relying too much on evidence of acts of bad temper that occurred up to five years ago. He pointed out that Brewer recollected only one instance of Mrs Knight being threatened, and he lived with them, unlike Mrs Collins whose evidence was questionable. What was the motive, he asked? Surely not the throwing of a cup of tea over him? Knight was not so drunk that he could not tell the difference between right and wrong. He said that there was a vast difference in meaning between the words 'That shall be the last cup of tea you shall throw at me,' and 'You shall not throw any more tea at me.' The exact words used were uncertain and there was no threat implied in the second expression. If Knight was incensed why did he not shoot his wife immediately instead of going outside and thinking about it for two or three minutes?

Bullen then demonstrated to the jury how Knight in trying to close the kitchen door would have had to raise the gun on his other arm and stick the muzzle through the half-open door, thereby accidentally discharging it. Why, asked Bullen, did Brewer on seeing the muzzle of the gun pointing at Mrs Knight not call out? (The poor boy was probably transfixed – it was not every day he saw a gun aimed at his stepmother.) Bullen referred to the fact that Knight immediately went away, no doubt horrified by what he had done. (The judge had something to say about this in his summing up.) Finally he asked the jury whether the fate of the accused should rest on the evidence of a fifteen-year-old boy who had changed his statement on each of his three visits to the witness-box. He ended by calling two more witnesses, who testified to Knight's good character and his lack of bad temper.

Judge Grantham began his summing up by reflecting on the circumstances in which Mrs Knight was killed and the possibility that it was an accident. He asked the jury to think of any way in which they could reconcile the facts with anything other than deliberate intent, and if they could do so it would be their duty to return a verdict accordingly, but if the facts pointed conclusively to a desire on Knight's part to kill his wife then it was their painful duty to return a verdict of guilty. He pointed out that there was very little evidence; in fact he could not remember a murder case in which there had been so little evidence. The prosecution relied to some extent on the evidence of ill-feeling between the couple but in his opinion that was not so important as it would have been if the defence had been one of manslaughter. He dismissed the evidence given by witnesses regarding incidents of bad temper as meaning nothing. All that could be said was that over the years Knight had used unkind words and bad language when the worse for drink, and maybe once or twice had hit Mrs Knight, but otherwise he had been a good husband.

The judge therefore asked the jury to forget anything that may have happened prior to that fateful evening. They should also not place too much reliance on the supposed words of the accused after the tea-throwing episode but concentrate on what happened afterwards. Was it not strange that Knight should choose that particular moment to fire off the bullets in his gun? There was no need for him to discharge the gun to get rid of the bullets – all he had to do was extract the cartridges from the breech. He asked the jury to consider whether it was possible for the gun to have gone off in the manner described and if so then they should give Knight the benefit of the doubt. Mr Bullen had said that it was common knowledge that one barrel of a gun would go off after the discharge of the other barrel. That might have been true once but with breech-loaders it was not so. It seemed to him almost impossible for the gun to have gone off accidentally. If the jury came to the conclusion that Knight in his anger deliberately fired the gun at his wife then it was their duty to find him guilty. The act of running away was not the conduct one would expect from a man who had just shot his wife by accident – he did not stop to see whether she was dead.

The jury reached their verdict within ten minutes without even retiring. The following exchanges then ensued. Foreman of the jury: 'We find him guilty, that he shot her during a fit of temper, and we strongly recommend him to mercy.' Clerk of assizes: 'Do you mean you find him guilty of murder?' Foreman : 'Of wilfully shooting her.' Judge: 'Perhaps you will say what you wish – you find the prisoner guilty of murder with a strong recommendation to mercy.' Foreman: 'That's what we mean, my lord.'

Asked whether he had anything to say, Knight replied, 'It went off accidentally.' The judge donned his black cap and told Knight that no-one who had heard the evidence could doubt that the verdict was a correct one. That an act was committed in a fit of passion or under the influence of drink was no excuse. If that were so the lives of half the population would be at risk. He pronounced sentence of death by hanging. Knight left the dock in a dazed condition. Had he really expected that people would believe his story and that he would get away with it? We shall never know.

'HAVE YOU HEARD OF A MURDER AT SOUTHAMPTON?'

On the afternoon of Wednesday 19 February 1896 eleven-year-old Sarah Philpott paid one of her frequent visits to her neighbour Mrs Angelina Faithfull, whom she called Mrs Burden because the man living with her was Frederick Burden. Sarah was in the habit of calling on Mrs Faithfull to assist her with odd jobs and errands. The house, No. 9 Brooklyn Road, Portswood, Southampton, was one of eight or nine similar houses in a terrace that backed on to the railway. Brooklyn Road was not then in what would be called today a 'nice' neighbourhood. There were unfinished houses opposite No. 9, sometimes occupied by tramps. It is a respectable area today and Brooklyn Road has been renamed Belgrave Road. It is now separated from the railway by Thomas Lewis Way.

Sarah found Mrs Faithfull and Burden in the front bedroom quarrelling, which apparently was nothing unusual in the three months they had been living together. (Mrs Faithfull had left her husband in August 1893.) She seemed to be much the worse for drink and was doing most of the talking. Sarah had earlier seen her coming from the direction of the nearest public house. The little girl stayed there for about two hours, until she was called home by her sister. The next day at about 1 pm Sarah called again at No. 9. She could not get in at the front door so entered the house by the back door. In the front bedroom she found Mrs Faithfull lying on the bed,with blood on her face and the bedclothes. She ran out screaming to tell her mother what she had seen. Two neighbours, Mrs Nicholls and Mr Murray, went to the bedroom to see for themselves and immediately sent for the police.

Inspector Hurst was the first on the scene. He found Mrs Faithfull lying on her left side facing the window with her throat cut. She was holding a razor between the finger and thumb of her right hand with the blade, which was covered in blood, turned away from her. Dr Ives the surgeon arrived soon afterwards and examined the wound. He found that her throat had been cut so deeply that the neck-bone had been severed.

On the Saturday evening Detective Inspector Boggeln went to the house in Middle Street that he knew to be the home of Burden's father. He found young Burden there, called him outside, and charged him with the murder of Mrs Faithfull. Burden said, 'I am not guilty. I was on the bridge at Winchester near the barracks at nine o'clock Thursday morning.' He said that he heard of the murder by reading of it in a newspaper at Salisbury and walked back to Southampton to give himself up in order to clear his name and help the police.

The trial of Frederick Burden began on Monday 29 June under Mr Justice Day. When the court opened the public gallery, said the *Southern Echo*, was 'literally stormed' and 'exciting struggles' took place for seats. Many women and young children were present, no doubt finding it a rare occasion to enliven their otherwise somewhat drab lives. Burden, looking very pale, pleaded 'Not Guilty'.

Mr C.T. Giles, the prosecuting counsel, reviewed the circumstances of the crime at some length and outlined the evidence connecting Burden with the murder. He said that Burden had gone to work at the docks on the Wednesday morning but had returned home very soon. Early the next day he was seen a short distance from Brooklyn Road and later that day making his way towards Winchester and Salisbury. He concluded his opening remarks by saying that there was no direct evidence to incriminate Burden, but asked why he should have left home and gone away at the very time that the crime was committed.

The first witness was young Sarah Philpott. She related the details of her visit to No. 9 on the Wednesday and the discovery of the body on the Thursday. She was asked whether other men visited the house when Burden was not there. At first she replied, 'Not that I know of,' then changed it to, 'Yes, but not very often.'

Inspector Hurst was asked about the state of Mrs Faithfull's clothes when her body was found and the amount of blood on them. He said that she was fully clothed up to her waist and was wearing a vest above the waist, and that she was covered by a sheet, a blanket and a quilt. There was one pillow under her head and that was saturated with blood. There was also blood on the sheets under and over her. A towel lying on the bed was also bloodstained as if it had been used for wiping away blood. Her head was hanging over the side of the bed and there was a great deal of blood on the floor. There were also spots of blood in other parts of the room, close to the fireplace and in a bucket of water on the floor.

Dr Ives described Mrs Faithfull's wound. He said that it could have been done by the razor she was holding but that she could not herself have done it, and therefore the razor had been placed in her hand by whoever had killed her. There were several bruises on parts of her body and she had been dead twelve or fourteen hours when he arrived. When he examined Burden after his arrest he found wounds in his throat such as would have been caused by a sharp instrument, and not as Burden had said through falling over a barbed-wire fence. He found bloodstains on both of the prisoner's sleeves and on his shirt, and in his opinion the amount of blood on his clothes could not have come solely from the wounds in his neck.

Annie Nicholls the neighbour described relations between Burden and Mrs Faithfull. Three weeks before the murder she had visited No. 9 and found Mrs Faithfull gasping for breath. 'Have you been hitting her?' she asked Burden. 'No,' he replied. Later Mrs Faithfull said to her, 'I shall have to leave Fred.' 'If you do you will go a limb short,' said Burden menacingly. A few days later she again visited No. 9 and found the couple at home. 'Fred has been trying to strangle me,' said Mrs Faithfull. 'Not only that but he has been trying to poison me.' In reply Burden poured himself two glasses of beer, drank them straight off and said, 'This will show you whether it is poison or not.' A few minutes later he was violently sick. All three then went to the local public house. When they parted afterwards Burden walked away in the direction of Swaythling as if he did not intend to return. Mrs Nicholls said that in between leaving her husband and meeting Burden Mrs Faithfull led an 'immoral' life but did not elaborate on that.

Stephen Paddick, a woodman, said that he saw a man, whom he now recognized as the prisoner, crossing a field near Romsey at about 7 am on Friday 21 February. Burden asked him whether he had a light. They walked along together for some distance and Burden asked, 'Have you heard of a murder at Southampton?' Paddick replied, 'No.' Burden then asked whether they were on the Salisbury road and walked off in that direction.

Giles, summing up for the prosecution, said that there could be no doubt that Burden had threatened Mrs Faithfull and that they were always quarrelling. He pointed out that Burden was with her at 7 pm on the Wednesday and that the murder was committed between then and about midnight. There was no suggestion that she had met anyone else later that evening. The amount of blood on Burden's clothes could not have come from the small wounds in his neck. Early on the Thursday morning a witness had seen Burden about 500 yards from the house. On the Friday morning when Burden met Paddick the woodman he asked him about the murder and could have known about it only from personal knowledge. He had told Inspector Boggeln that he first knew of the murder when he saw a newspaper placard on the Friday at Salisbury that read, 'Sad fate of a woman.'

With that evidence he said that the jury must find the prisoner guilty.

Mr E.U. Bullen, the defence counsel, said that the case rested entirely on circumstantial evidence, and that it was very weak evidence. He said that Burden had been a respectable and hard-working young man until he met Mrs Faithfull, who had left her husband in 1893 in order to live the life of a prostitute. She had persuaded Burden to live with her and in consequence he had become an outcast from his family and friends. There was no evidence to prove that he had committed the murder. Mrs Faithfull had encouraged men to visit her and that had resulted in frequent quarrels. Who could say with certainty that someone else had not been there that evening? No-one knew what had happened and no-one saw anything. Could they convict Burden with this lack of evidence? She was holding Burden's razor, but that was the only weapon to hand in the room and the natural one for a murderer to use. He pointed out that the lamp in the room had been left burning. Surely if Burden was the murderer he would have put out the light to avert suspicion? He said that Burden could have seen a newspaper placard before meeting the woodman and not read the full details until he got to Salisbury. When he found out that Mrs Faithfull was the victim he returned to Southampton to clear himself from suspicion. (Bullen did not mention the fact that Burden did not give himself up – he waited for the police to find him.) He said that it was a pity that Burden was not permitted to give evidence on his own behalf, otherwise he might have been able to clear himself. (It was to be another two years before the law was changed in this respect.)

The judge in his summing up said that just because the victim appeared to be a loose woman it did not exonerate the murderer. That it was murder and not suicide had been made clear, and deliberate murder at that. The question for the jury to resolve was whether on reasonable grounds they were convinced that Burden was the murderer. He referred to his statement that he was at Winchester at 9 am on the Thursday. What was he doing there? Another witness had seen him at Portswood at about the same time. Who was telling the truth? If the jury had any reasonable doubt it was for them to say that the prisoner was not guilty. In view of what happened next it would seem that the jury were not helped by the judge's summing up.

After the jury had retired for three hours the judge, perhaps becoming impatient, sent for them. The foreman said that they could not agree. The judge asked him whether they were likely to agree and had they thoroughly discussed the matter? 'Is there any hope of your agreeing?' he asked. 'Would another hour help you?' The foreman replied not even if they stopped there all night. The judge therefore discharged the jury. The next morning Judge Day announced that he would hold a new trial the very next day, Wednesday, with a new jury, as nothing would be gained by postponing it to the next assizes. Mr Bullen said that the prisoner wanted the case to be cleared up as soon as possible.

When the new trial began Giles for the prosecution stated the facts as given at the first trial, with one or two new points, such as the house being completely unfurnished with the exception of the front bedroom, and that Mrs Faithfull was often seen to be drunk. The witnesses for the prosecution gave the same evidence as at the first trial. This time, however, the clothes worn by Mrs Faithfull when she was killed were displayed to the jury together with the coat Burden was wearing when arrested. Inspector Boggeln said that the 4.30 pm edition of the *Southern Echo* on Thursday 20 February contained a report of the murder. Giles pointed out that this was relevant to Burden's question to Paddick the following morning. Had Burden seen a copy of that paper in his wanderings? If not and he was innocent, how did he know there had been a murder? Obviously by the fact that he himself had committed the murder. Bullen for the defence answered this point by suggesting that Burden had either seen a newspaper placard with a headline about the murder or heard a newsboy shouting something about a murder. When he read the details at Salisbury he hurried back to Southampton. Would a guilty man have returned to the scene of his crime?

The judge in his summing up said that the evidence was circumstantial but that the jury should not be misled by that word. In all such cases the evidence was more or less circumstantial. They had to use their judgement and discretion, and if they succeeded in drawing their inferences correctly then they had done their duty. It had been said that the prisoner was very fond of the dead woman, but all the evidence suggested otherwise, and that she had been subjected to considerable cruelty. There was no evidence that other men were visiting her. (But Sarah Philpott had said so, and so had Bullen.) The evidence was that Burden had at least once tried to strangle her, and the bruises on her body were unaccounted for. He said that Burden was the last person seen with her while she was still alive. (If he meant that remark to count against Burden it was directly opposed to what he had said in the James Parker trial, that because a person was the last to be seen with the victim it did not necessarily incriminate that person.) The jury had seen the clothes worn by Burden – there were blood marks all over them. It was for the jury to consider how that much blood came upon his clothes. He found it strange that the prisoner should go away just when the woman was found dead, and why was he wandering about the countryside unless he was guilty of the murder and dared not go back. In conclusion the judge asked the jury to consider the case as 'common-sense business men' and arrive at a conclusion that they believed would be a just and right one.

When the jury retired there was intense speculation in court as to the outcome of the trial. Would the jury again disagree? This time the jury returned after only half an hour. The foreman announced that they were agreed on a verdict of 'Guilty', but they recommended that the prisoner be shown mercy on account of his age (twenty-three) and the character of Mrs Faithfull. Burden, asked whether he had anything to say, replied, 'All I can say is that I did not do it.' The judge passed sentence of death. Burden was executed on 21 July 1896. How was it that one jury retired for three hours without coming to a decision, and another jury reviewing the same evidence came to a decision in half an hour? There is no answer to that. All that can be said perhaps is that the jury system is not such a good institution as many people believe. Was Burden guilty? Almost certainly, but there is no record of whether he admitted his guilt while awaiting execution. When a prisoner continues to protest his innocence it always raises a slight doubt in one's mind.

MURDER AT THE POST OFFICE

Flora Timms, who later became famous under her married name of Flora Thompson, the author of the trilogy *Lark Rise to Candleford*, came to Grayshott in the north-east of Hampshire in 1897 at the age of twenty to work at the post office in Crossways Road. She lodged at first with Walter Chapman, the postmaster, and his family and later moved to lodgings in the village. At that date several famous people lived in the district and the post office was used by George Bernard Shaw and Arthur Conan Doyle among others. Shaw rented a house in the village named Blencathra (later St Edmund's school) from 1898 to 1900, and Doyle lived at Hindhead from 1898 to 1908. After four years at Grayshott Flora Timms left to get married. She returned to Hampshire in 1916 when her husband became the postmaster at Liphook.

Grayshott in 1901 was a fairly prosperous place. There were large villas in and around the village and the shops were larger and more varied than in the average Hampshire village. Most of the houses were of nineteenth-century date and the church was built in that very year. Land had greatly increased in value over the last few years and many residents had made money by investing in land and property. It was thought at one time that Grayshott would become a sizeable town but it never achieved its full potential and lost out to Haslemere and Hindhead. It was part of Headley parish then but became a separate parish in 1902 because the residents wanted a piped water supply and Headley residents did not. The post office was sufficiently busy and profitable, because there was no post office at Hindhead, to require two young female assistants. It was situated on the southwest side of Crossways Road not far from the village centre. It was demolished in 1986 and replaced by a building named Pendarvis.

Walter Chapman, a joiner and cabinet-maker by trade, had been appointed postmaster about nine years ago, having previously worked for his brother Ernest, a partner in a local building firm. He had a workshop in part of the post office building where he carried on his trade. One year after his appointment he married Emily, she being seven years younger than Walter and said to have been his housekeeper. She also had a brother who owned a prosperous business in Grayshott. Chapman was now forty-five years old and his wife thirty-eight, and there were five children, the eldest being six years old and the youngest only six or seven weeks old. It was well known in the village that it was not a happy marriage, one of the reasons being that Chapman was obsessively, almost pathologically, jealous of his wife, but there was no foundation for his belief that she consorted with other men.

One day early in the year Chapman's brother Ernest called on the Chapmans while they were in the middle of a dreadful quarrel. Chapman was acting and speaking like a madman and calling his wife all sorts of unprintable names. He accused her of immoral behaviour with 'men who had been around the house all night'. Ernest told him not to treat his wife like that and said that he was suffering from a delusion as he had never proved his wife guilty, and even if it were true he had no right to speak like that and it would be better for them to separate. He quoted from the Bible, 'Vengeance is mine, saith the Lord, I will repay.' 'It is in His hands,' said Ernest. 'It is not for you to visit it on your wife.' Walter hesitated then said to his wife, 'That is the very text that saved you from having a bullet through you.' (He was said to be an atheist.)

Relations between the couple became so strained that soon after this incident Mrs Chapman ran away with the children to her brother-in-law's house. Chapman said then that he would not have her back. To everybody's surprise she returned in May and there was a reconciliation. Recently she had been heard to say that the two months since returning home had been among the happiest days of her married life. (Although that may not have been saying very much, if the rest of her married life is anything to go by.) Her youngest child must have been born soon after returning to her husband.

On Monday 29 July at about 9.45 am the quiet of the post office was broken by screams in the living-room at the rear of the building. Annie Harding, the Chapmans' maidservant, who was upstairs getting fresh clothes for the baby that Mrs Chapman was bathing in the living-room, heard the children crying and rushed downstairs. There she saw Mr Chapman struggling with his wife as he bent over her holding some sort of sharp implement. Staying only long enough to pick up the baby she noticed blood on Mrs Chapman's clothes before running out into the road, where she was joined by the two young post office assistants who were screaming for help.

Gilbert Winchester, an apprentice in Chapman's joinery business, ran into the living-room when he heard screams but was so frightened by what he saw that he immediately ran out into the road, where he met Ernest Chapman. The latter ran in and found Mrs Chapman lying on the floor covered in blood and groaning; he raised her up but after a few seconds she became quiet and lifeless. Arnold Lyndon, the local doctor, soon arrived and examined the dead

THE MURDERER IS A HERO

*Buckingham House, where the Duke of Buckingham
was murdered in 1628.*

*Memorial to the Duke of
Buckingham in
Portsmouth cathedral.*

THE GENUINE
HISTORY
Of the Inhuman and Unparalell'd
MURDERS
Committed on the BODIES of
Mr. WILLIAM GALLEY,
A Custom-House Officer in the Port of *Southampton*. And
Mr. DANIEL CHATER,
A Shoemaker, of *Fordingbridge* in *Hampshire*.

TOGETHER WITH

An Account of the Trials of the **Seven Bloody Criminals**, at CHICHESTER, by Virtue of a Special Commission, on the 16th, 17th and 18th of *January* 1748: By which it appears, there never was such a Horrible Scene of Villainy ever heard of or known in the World before.

With a Particular Account of their Behaviour while under Confinement at *Chichester*, both before, at, and after Sentence of Death was pass'd upon them: Together with their Dying Words and Behaviour at the Place of Execution, which was at 3 o'Clock, on *Thursday*, *Jan.* 19. 1748-9.

Written by a GENTLEMAN at *Chichester*;
And Publish'd at the Request of the Gentlemen of the County of *Sussex*; in Order to prevent the World from being amus'd with false and fictitious Relations.

LONDON:

Printed for the Proprietor, and published by B. DICKINSON, at the Corner of the *Bell-Savage Inn*, *Ludgate-Hill*. 1749. [Price Six Pence.]

This Pamphlet is entered in the Hall-Book of the Company of Stationers, and at the Stamp-Office; and whoever shall presume to pyrate it, or any Part thereof, will be prosecuted as the Law directs.

'THROW HIM DOWN THE WELL'
The book written soon after the trial of the smugglers.

MURDERED BY SOLDIERS
Memorial to Thomas Webb at Curdridge.

TRIALS FOR MURDER.

This Day is Published, Price 3d.

THE TRIAL

OF

JAMES COLLOPPY, JOHN DIGGENS,
and RICHARD PENDERGRASS,

FOR THE

INHUMAN MURDER

OF

THOMAS WEBB,

At Bishop's Waltham, in this County.

To which is added,

THE TRIAL OF JUAN BARUCO,

For the Murder of

ANTONIO LUCENA.

Printed and Sold by B. LONG, at the Hampshire Chronicle Office, Cathedral-Yard, Winton; sold also by Matthews, Portsmouth; Holmes, Droxford; Seagrave, Chichester; Rooke, Southampton; Albin, Newport, Salter, Ryde, and Combes, Cowes, Isle of Wight; Matthews, Basingstoke; Hollis, Romsey; Richardson, Petersfield; Abbett, Lymington; Corfe, Stockbridge; Easton, Salisbury; Roe, Alton; Collington, Alresford, Cook, Farnham; Cook, Godalming; Jennings, Bishop's Waltham; and may be had of the Newsmen.

The report of the trial of the murderers of Thomas Webb.

'KILLED A YOUNG GIRL. IT WAS FINE AND HOT'.
Tanhouse Lane, Alton, today.

Grave of Fanny Adams.

Contemporary record of Baker's execution.

THE MURDER OF JAMES PARKER
Gravestone of James Parker at Kings Worthy.

'YOU SHALL NOT THROW ANY MORE TEA AT ME'
Cricketers Cottage after its closure as an inn.

Cricketers Cottage today.

Shocking Tragedy at Portswood.

WOMAN FOUND DEAD.

HEAD ALMOST SEVERED FROM THE BODY.

A GHASTLY SCENE.

Southampton is very fortunate in not having many tragedies, but when they do occur, they are generally of a very sad nature. The inhabitants of Portswood were greatly alarmed to-day to hear that a tragedy

HAVE YOU HEARD OF A MURDER AT SOUTHAMPTON?
Headlines of the Burden murder. (Southern Echo).

MURDER AT THE POST OFFICE
*The Fox and Pelican public house, Grayshott,
where the Chapman inquest was held.*

'I HAVE JUST KILLED A MAN'
Hindhead Chase (formerly Arundel), Grayshott.

TRIP WITH TOPLIS.

Loaded Revolver in the Car.

YOUNG PRIVATE CHARGED AT ANDOVER.

Didn't Know of Murder Till He Saw Papers.

At Andover to-day Harry Fallows, a private soldier, aged 19, was remanded, charged with on April 24th, receiving, harbouring, and maintaining one Percy Toplis, who had lately before committed the crime of murder, and with knowing that Toplis had committed the said crime.

Accused, who is boyish-looking, appeared in no way perturbed when the charge was read over to him. He made no statement.

The clerk of the court read the evidence given by Superintendent Cox, who was unable to be present. The superintendent said at 11.15 on Tuesday he saw prisoner at Bulford. He said he told prisoner he believed he knew something, and Fallows replied: "Yes, I know Toplis. I saw him on Saturday afternoon, and about eleven that night he came to the cookhouse door in a motor car, and he promised me a ride, and I went with him on a run down to Wales. He had a loaded revolver with him, but I did not know what had happened until I had read it in the papers. I am glad I am able to inform you something."

Funeral of the Victim.

The funeral of Sidney George Spicer, the victim of the Thruxton Down murder, took place at the London-road Cemetery, Salisbury, yesterday afternoon in the presence of a large gathering. The Rev. J. W. O. Wand, Vicar of St. Mark's, conducted the service.

In addition to the family mourners there were also present representatives of the four local lodges of the R.A.O.B., of which Order the deceased was a member, and also a large number of licensed motor drivers, bearing a handsome wreath in the shape of a motor wheel. At the conclusion of the ordinary service the Buffalo form of service was read by Bro. Barber, R.O.H., the various members linking hands round the grave in the customary manner. The coffin bore the following inscription:

SIDNEY GEORGE SPICER,
Died April 24, 1920,
Aged 29 years.

KILLER ON THE RUN
Headlines of the Toplis murder. (Southern Daily Echo).

THE PORTSEA CRIME.

Detained Man Released at Portsmouth.

BLOODHOUNDS MYTH

No Truth They Have Been Used.

REVENGE THE MOTIVE?

We were officially informed at the Town Hall this morning that there is no truth in the story that has gained currency in the London Press that bloodhounds were yesterday employed to assist in solving the mystery of the Blossom Alley murder. The story was the outcome of a rumour which originated in Queen Street yesterday afternoon, and so quickly did it spread throughout the district, that within a very short time there had collected in Cross Street and North Street, at the two ends of Blossom Alley, a large crowd of curious spectators. The bloodhounds, however, did not appear. "The idea was absurd," said an official this morning. "To have employed bloodhounds so long after the crime would have been futile."

Statements by Women.

Yesterday the detectives were busily engaged taking statements from a number of women who were acquainted with the deceased woman. A man was also brought in and closely questioned. He was subsequently kept at the police station pending further interrogation this morning, after which he was released. We understand that the reason the man was detained at the police station all night was that the police were dissatisfied with a statement that he made. This man was a well-known character in the Portsea district, and was known amongst the women of Mary Pelham's class.

Excitement continues high in Portsea where the continued presence of detectives, police officers, Pressmen and photographers arouses curiosity, and knots of men and women are almost constantly to be seen standing at either end of Blossom Alley.

The impression prevails that the murderer will be found amongst the civilian class, and the suggestion was this morning advanced to our representative by a person living in the neighbourhood of the crime that a woman may have been involved in the murder. "There are women as well as men in some of these places who would stop at nothing," said our informant.

That the police expect to find the culprit amongst the civilian population is seen in the fact that a very close watch was this morning kept upon the Public Gallery at the Police Court where doubtful characters, very often spend an hour or two feasting their eyes on the misery of others. In this close scrutiny the police had civilian assistance.

No Money or Jewellery.

We understand that neither jewellery nor money were found in the deceased woman's house. Not infrequently the woman wore several rings, but they were not of much value. From time to time, when short of a few shillings, she would pawn a ring or two and redeem them when in funds. It is known that on Friday she had very little money indeed. When women of this class are at the lowest ebb financially, the fact is always known by her associates, so that the theory that she was murdered by someone in the locality from a motive of robbery can be discounted. Rather, perhaps, was it a motive of revenge.

Another point that leads to the assumption that the criminal is a civilian is the fact that the

---

MURDER IN BLOSSOM ALLEY
Headlines of the Pelham murder. (Evening News).

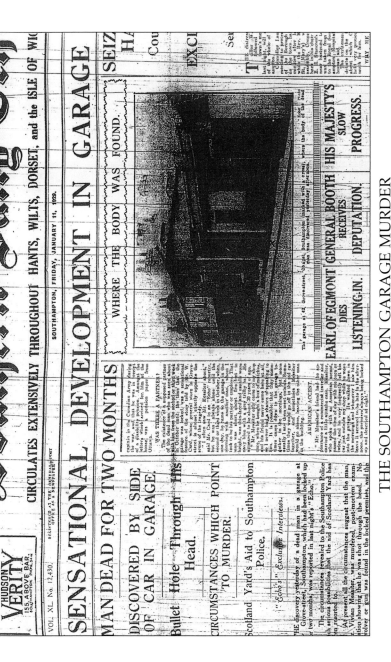

THE SOUTHAMPTON GARAGE MURDER

Headlines of the Southampton garage murder. (Southern Daily Echo).

'Case Against Pye Would Be Funny If It Were Not So Serious'

ANOTHER MAN MURDERED YVONNE (CLAIM DEFENCE)

'THE defence say that Pye was not the man. There was another man'. This claim was put forward by Mr. David Croom-Johnson, Q.C., at Hampshire Assizes yesterday, where he is defending 27-year-old farm-worker Derek Pye, charged with murdering 14-year-old schoolgirl Yvonne Laker, on a train near Basingstoke on June 29. The prosecution's case against Pye opened on Monday and ended at 11.15 yesterday morning.

After the prosecution's case had finished the jury of nine men and three women filed out while a submission was made by Mr. Croom-Johnson.

On their return Mr. Croom-Johnson said "The prosecution say that Pye is the man who committed the murder. They say that for one reason and for one reason only. They reason in this way—'You were on the train, Yvonne Laker was on the train. You and Yvonne Laker were in the same coach when it left Winchester. When it got to Basingsoke she was dead. There was nobody else on the coach and nobody else could possibly have killed her'.

"That is the whole basis of their claim."

He went on "The defence say that Pye was not the man. There was another man. The prosecution say this second man never existed—unknown, unseen, untraced. Until Pye went to the police and said 'I was there', the police had not even got as far as the first man. If this situation was not so serious it would be almost funny. He is somebody who gives all this information to the police and finishes up as the man charged with the murder—It's ironic."

Mr. Croom-Johnson said he would be calling the evidence of a signalman in the box controlling the out home signal who would say that on two occasions, at two places, the train was signalled down in such a way its speed was reduced—unlike the evidence of the guard—to a walking pace.

'SAW A MAN'

Mr. Croom-Johnson said a lady working by a window of the Eli Lilly factory near the station saw, just after the passage of a train, a man walking along the track from Basingstoke station. And he was not a railwayman.

Down by the signal post there were some railway workers. Just after the murder train went through a man came towards them from the direction of Basingstoke along the lines. He acted "rather suspiciously" and appeared disconcerted when he saw the railwaymen. He went towards Winchester for some distance and then turned north away from the railway line. He was hurrying and going at a good speed.

"Finally," said Mr. Croom-Johnson to the jury, "there is a road to the north and a man who may well have been this man was seen hiding in some bushes. What do you think about that? Might that have been a man who dropped off the train when it slowed down by the home signal?

TRAIN JOURNEY

Pye, who went into the dock yesterday afternoon, described in a clear, quiet voice, his train journey from Winchester to Basingstoke the afternoon schoolgirl Yvonne Laker was murdered—a crime to which Pye pleads not guilty.

Pye said that when he got on the train he noticed a man and a young girl in the compartment. They were sitting about half way down the coach, facing the back of the coach. The train started and the first stop was Micheldever.

"I went to the toilet not very long after leaving Winchester and when the train stopped at Micheldever was still in there. When it restarted I came out. Back in the coach a man was helping a girl—they were in the gangway. The girl was nearest the nearside and he had his left arm round her shoulder. His other arm was near her right arm. Her head was slightly down and I couldn't see her face properly.

Pye said he asked the man what was wrong and got a reply 'She's been sick'. He held the door open for the man and girl to pass through. He did not see them together again. A few minutes later the man came out and sat near the window on the nearside in the first section of the compartment.

"I asked him if the young girl was all right and he said 'yes'. I asked him if there was anything I could do and he said 'You can

read his paper. The man came down the gangway soon after Pye sat down, got about half way, saw Pye and then went back.

"I did not see him again. The train arrived at Basingstoke. I went down the platform and through the barrier. I said I had not got a ticket, put two shillings on the barrier and said 'That should cover it'."

CYCLED HOME

He did not go into the bus station cafe but after a drink and finding he had missed a bus, caught a train to Hook, where he took a taxi to Odiham, cycling home from there to Long Sutton.

"When I read in the paper on the Tuesday about the murder I did not connect it with what happened to me on the train the day before. It said the train was crowded but the train I was on was not crowded."

On the following Friday when waiting in a cell to appear at Aldershot magistrates court on a motor car offence he told P.c. Eggleton he had been on a train where he had seen some broken glass.

"I had heard police constables on the Friday morning talking about broken glass." (Case continued.

FIRST DAY

When the hearing opened on Monday morning Pye, smartly dressed in a light grey suit, entered a plea of "not guilty" to murdering Yvonne on June 29 when she was returning to boarding school after a weekend visit to her grandparents at Barton-on-Sea.

Retracing the girl's train journey from Southampton, Mr. Jeremy Hutchinson, Q.C., for the prosecution, said that she was seen sitting in her seat at Winchester by a porter.

"From the moment the train left Winchester, she was not seen again by anybody until her body was found at Basingstoke," he said. "It was during the 24 minutes between Winchester and Basingstoke that this crime was perpetrated."

At Basingstoke a number of people got into the murder coach, including a young schoolboy, the court was told. It was he who discovered the girl's mutilated body and raised the alarm, shortly after the train left Basingstoke.

The police arrived on the scene to find the girl's body in the lavatory compartment. She was wearing no shoes and her beret was missing, said Mr. Hutchinson.

"Her throat had been cut and there was very substantial bleeding," he continued. "There was no sign of any weapon at all."

Most vigorous inquiries were set afoot, he went on. "As you will appreciate, when such a crime is perpetrated—in a public place and without any apparent direct motive—no more difficult possible investigation can confront the police."

A report of a post mortem stated that the girl had been struck a blow, with some violence, on the side of her head. It also appeared, from medical evidence, that her breathing had been obstructed, by placing a hand over her nose and mouth. This could have been to prevent shouting or noise, suggested Mr. Hutchinson.

Giving details of glass found by police alongside the railway track and in the girl's clothing Mr. Hutchinson said that these had been fitted together to form the bottom half of a sherry bottle, similar to one which Pye is alleged to have admitted buying in Basingstoke some hours after the girl was murdered.

(Continued on Page 12)

The Night He Took a Turn on the Footplate

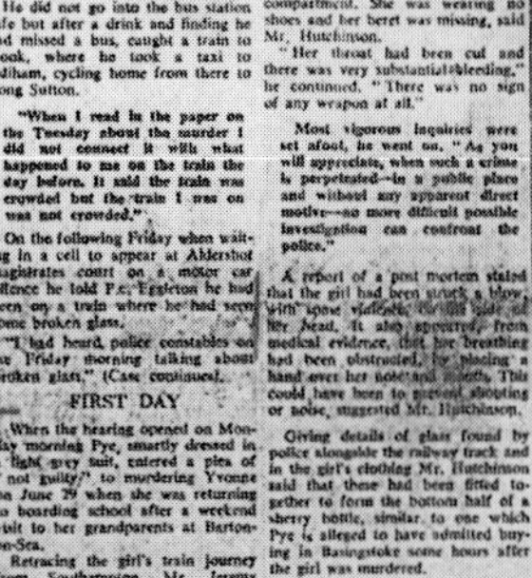

A keen railway enthusiast all his life, Mr. J. Hughes at work on one of his model engines—on Tuesday evening he was working on a much larger, engine when he 'stood in' on the footplate for an injured fireman and helped bring the 6 p.m. train from Wimbledon to Basingstoke.

IT was back to the footplate for Mr. John Hughes, of 73 Penrith Road, Basingstoke, clerk in the British Railways headquarters offices at Marylebone and former fireman at Stevens

hospital.

"We were so long in the station I realised something was wrong," said Mr. Hughes, "so I got off the train to have a look. When I heard we were

Roman Tomb Installed in Museum

The three-ton Roman tomb—unearthed at the Winklebury housing site during roadwork July—was installed at Basingstoke museum yesterday afternoon. The tomb will stand in entrance hall of the building in New Street. Later on, when a specially designed glass c can be fitted as protection, the human bones taken out of the coffin, will be laid in it once m

Hook Man Sent For Trial on Armed Robbery Charge

LADY Margaret Cornwallis of Castle Mill House, North Warnborough, described at Aldershot Magistrates Court on Wednesday how a masked man, armed with a pistol, entered her home, told her he was desperate and forced her to hand over £4.10.0.

After leaving the house, he put the gun through the opening of a door which was on a chain, Lady Cornwallis told the court. She said she was frightened and locked herself in an upstairs room.

The alleged intruder, James Kimber (34), who was lodging at the time at 39 Carleton Close, Hook, and now described as of no fixed address, was sent for trial at Wiltshire Assizes, which open at Devizes on January 11. Through Mr. G. R. Beeley he pleaded not guilty and reserved his defence. He was granted a defence certificate but bail was refused.

Lady Cornwallis, an elderly widow, said in her evidence that she was alone at the time, about 7 p.m. on November 3 and had just finished supper in the study. She thought all the doors were locked but heard a bang from the back of the house. As she opened the study door she was confronted by a man holding a gun and he pushed her back into the room.

'FACE COVERED'

The man, who was wearing a dark coat and had his face covered halfway up with some darkish material, told her he was desperate and must have money. She told him she did not keep a lot in the house and he said "You must have a lot of money. You must be rich. It is a big house.

Sitting down she turned out her two handbags, said Lady Cornwallis. One was empty and the other contained four £1 notes and about 10/- in change. The man, who was wearing gloves, took the money after she had said "You had better take it if you want it."

"He was standing near me holding a gun by my face," said Lady Cornwallis. "He told me he had been at 'The Moor' doing five years but I did not believe it.

"He made me promise not to ring up the police that night and we shook hands on it. He did not seem in a hurry to go and I told him 'If you are on the run you had better go quickly.'

"Finally he went out through the back door. I slammed it and locked it. I felt very frightened then. I went into the sitting room and just at that minute the telephone rang. I found it was a neighbour and we

window to see if any policemen were coming."

Lady Cornwallis described the clothing worn by the man and said he spoke in a rather gentle, not strident voice. Later she pointed out Kimber at an identity parade as the man who had robbed her.

In cross-examination, Lady Cornwallis said she felt absolutely certain it was a pistol the man was holding. She finally recognised him when he read out passages at her request.

Charles Frederick Ruddock, of 16 Recreation Road, Odiham, said he saw Kimber in High Street, Odiham, just before 6 p.m. on November 3. Kimber, who appeared quite normal, said he hoped to go to see his mother some time that evening.

Mrs. Marjorie Parrack, Castle Mill Cottage, whose husband is gardener to Lady Cornwallis, said that at midday on November 4 she found a button in the grounds at the front of the house.

Mrs. Teresa Hooley, 39 Carleton Close, Hook, said a man telephoned for lodgings during the afternoon of November 3 and at 8.40 p.m. Kimber arrived and arranged to stay until the following Friday. He paid her £3.3.0 and she saw he was wearing a dark coat or poplin raincoat similar to the one in court.

RAINCOAT

Mrs. Ada Field, of 3 Cobbett Green Winchester Road, Basingstoke, senior sales assistant to W. H. Stevens, London Road, Basingstoke, said that on October 10 a man and woman who gave their names as Kimber and an address at Hook Caravan Site, approached her about opening a credit account. The man bought a raincoat identical to the one she had brought to court.

Det. Sgt. Leslie Bran said that when interviewed next day Kimber said, "Armed robbery? Not me. I know nothing about it." Asked where he was the previous evening Kimber said, "I was drinking in the morning in Basingstoke and bought two bottles of VP wine. I don't know what I did or where I went after that but I know I did not do any 'screwing.'"

When shown the button and asked how all the buttons came to be missing from his raincoat he said, "They got loose and came off at different times. I don't know where I lost them. When charged he said, "I don't know anything about it."

EVICTIONS DEPLORED

A RESOLUTION dep-
ing Basingstoke Boro
Council's action in ta
out eviction warrants ag
three local families came
fore the annual meeting
Basingstoke and Dis
Social Workers Group
night.

The resolution, which
be forwarded to the T
Clerk, said the Coun
action "suggests to u
misunderstanding of the
poses of municipal ho
and an abdication by
local authority of its
sponsibilities for
socially inadequate peo

MURDER ON THE TRAIN

Headlines of the train murder. (Hampshire Chronicle).

DEATH IN A TAXI

Newbery was murdered in this lane leading to Hawstead Farm.

Southern Evening ECHO

SOUTHAMPTON, THURSDAY, OCT. 22, 1964. Price 3d.

77th Year No. 22041

CITY FINAL

TAXI DRIVER MURDERED

Battered body of Soton man found in lane

"Echo" Crime Reporter

A MAN, believed to be a Southampton taxi driver, was found dead with his head battered in Hawstead-lane off the Chandler's Ford to Hursley road today.

It is thought he was a man aged about 64 in

Cabinet ponders Queen's speech

THE Government's economic situation was again discussed when the Cabinet met at 10 Downing-street, today.

Mr. Wilson, the Prime Minister, presided over what was the second meeting of his Cabinet. Between now and Monday the promised Government statement on the economic outlook will be issued.

Thought is also being given by the Cabinet to what will be in the Queen's Speech at the opening of the new Parliament on Tuesday week. A considerable programme is expected to be foreshadowed.

Weather in the South

As issued by the Meteorological Office, Southampton, at noon today. Tel 28841

FORECAST (3 p.m. to 6 a.m.): Rather cloudy but mainly dry, with a few sunny intervals, but cloudy by day, a period of rain during the night, followed by brighter, showery, occasional weather. Maximum temperature today about 12 degrees C (55 degrees F), falling to around 8 deg C (46 degrees F) tonight, with a fresh wind. Becoming fresh NW tomorrow morning.

OUTLOOK: 6 a.m. to 6 p.m. sunny periods and showers.

woman. He found several stab wounds to the chest near the heart. There was no sign of an implement or tool in the room that could have been used to inflict the injuries, but on further examination of the body he found embedded in her back to a depth of 4 inches a long fine metal blade, which he extricated with a pair of pincers. It was the blade of a cabinet-maker's carving tool; the handle was found later on the mantelpiece.

Police Constable Merritt found Chapman upstairs sitting calmly on his bed. 'What's up, Mr Chapman ?' said Merritt. 'Are you aware your wife is dead?' Chapman replied, 'I know. I did it. Take me away.' On being brought downstairs Chapman met his brother and said, 'Don't think too bad of me.' Ernest Chapman replied, 'Oh, brother, what did you do this for? You had no business to send her into eternity like that. Why did you not go away or send her away? There's nothing but the blood of Jesus can wash away the guilt of your crime. That is the one hope and the only hope there is for you now. Brother, if you had believed in the love of God you would never have done this. This is what your atheism has brought you to.' Walter Chapman made no reply.

Police Sergeant Nunn, summoned from Whitehill, charged Chapman with wilful murder, to which he replied, 'Quite right. I know I shall have to stand before my maker. My intention was to have blown my brains out and have settled the lot. I am only sorry that I have left my little children behind.' He was then taken to Alton police station. A large crowd remained outside the post office for the rest of the day. Nothing as tragic as this had happened at Grayshott within living memory.

On the following day Chapman was brought to court at Alton for a preliminary hearing. The magistrate committed him to Winchester prison on remand for a week. The inquest was held on the Wednesday at the Fox and Pelican public house at Grayshott, conducted by the county coroner, Henry White. The Fox and Pelican had a strange history. It was opened in 1899 by the Grayshott and District Refreshment Association with the intention of encouraging the sale of non-alcoholic drinks. It sold alcohol but only out of sight from under the counter. (It sold much more beer than soft drinks.) It was opened by the wife of the Bishop of Winchester so it had ecclesiastical blessing. Chapman declined to attend the inquest, for reasons best known to himself.

Ernest Chapman was closely questioned regarding relations between Walter and his wife, the coroner evidently trying to discover what if anything had provoked this savage attack after what had by all accounts been a peaceful two months reconciliation. He said that throughout the marriage there had been differences between them amounting at times to real unpleasantness and that he had been present at one 'terrible row' when Chapman had threatened to shoot her. He had to admit that he had not been aware of any quarrels during the last two months and that he had heard her say that they were getting on 'wonderfully well'. (She probably meant by comparison with before.)

Dr Lyndon in his evidence said that Mrs Chapman was dead by the time he arrived. The carving tool that he found embedded in her back had passed through the spinal column but that wound was not the cause of death. The stab-wounds to the chest had been inflicted with great force and two of those had penetrated to the heart vessels and had proved fatal.

The coroner in his summing up said that this was as painful a case as was possible for a jury to consider. The evidence was so clear-cut that there was little else to be said in the matter. He expressed his deep sympathy for the little children, now left all alone in the world. (He evidently saw no hope for Chapman.) All the jury needed to do was to satisfy themselves as to the cause of death and say whether that arose from the wilful act of another person. Whether Chapman was in his right mind was not for them to say – only to decide that he was or was not the guilty man and whether the act was deliberate, and unfortunately for Chapman the evidence was only too clear. The jury immediately returned a verdict of wilful murder against Walter Chapman.

Chapman was brought before the Alton magistrates again on the following Tuesday. Although the case was not to be heard until the afternoon he was brought to Alton by train early in the day and safely lodged at the police station to avoid trouble from onlookers. He was dressed in a grey suit and a soft felt hat. He was a small man weighing only 8 stones, thin-featured with dark hair and moustache. Three brothers of Chapman attended the court. He sat for most of the time with his eyes closed but was listening intently to the evidence.

No new evidence was forthcoming at the magistrates court. The same witnesses gave more or less the same evidence as at the inquest. Mr Jackson of Farnham, representing Chapman, said that the one question that might have to be determined, the state of the accused's mind, could not be decided at this hearing and he did not propose therefore to call any witnesses on behalf of Chapman. At the end the prisoner said, 'I call no witnesses, and I reserve my defence.'

The trial was held at Winchester in November. Mr Giles and Mr Charles prosecuted on behalf of the Crown, and Charles Mathews (who had been prosecuting counsel in the Kings Worthy murder case in 1886) appeared on behalf of Chapman. On being charged by the Clerk of Assize, Chapman replied, 'I am guilty of manslaughter, not of murder.' Mathews hastily rose to ask the judge to alter that to a plea of 'Not Guilty'. The trial lasted just an hour and a half.

Giles, in his opening address for the prosecution, said that there were circumstances connected with the case that might relieve the jury of some anxiety in coming to a verdict. He said it was the duty of the prosecution to enquire into the past history of the accused to see whether there was anything bearing on the case, and that had been done. As a result evidence would be presented as to the prisoner's state of mind. He said that Chapman had been suffering not only from delusions regarding his wife's morality, which were unfounded, but also from the delusion that he was being shadowed by detectives, also without foundation. In May of this year Chapman had sent a telegram to the Petersfield postmaster with the cryptic message 'Diabolical plot to ruin me'. If all those statements were proved it would be for the jury to decide on the state of the prisoner's mind at the time of the attack.

Ernest Chapman was called to give further evidence. He said that he had noticed for some three or four years past that his brother had been 'very strange in his manner'. A prominent delusion was that his wife had been unfaithful. He also thought that the children were not his children. He was also under the impression that there was a conspiracy against him and that he was watched by detectives everywhere he went. In May he had given Ernest an envelope marked 'To be opened in case of my death'. Mathews for the defence proposed to read out the document that was in the envelope but omitting the names of persons against whom false accusations had been made. It said that there was a conspiracy to ruin him (Chapman gave names) and it went on, 'Last but not least my late wife can answer this question.' Here Mathews pointed out the significance of the word 'late' written two months before he killed her. The text concluded, 'a woman deceitful and deep as hell... I was ignorant.' The rest of the document was in the form of a will.

Dr Lyndon gave evidence regarding Chapman's medical history. He said that Chapman had consulted him privately and Lyndon had come to the conclusion that either Chapman was suffering from delusions or his wife was a wicked woman, but most likely the former. Chapman told Lyndon that men came to the house at night, pulled the timber about and struck matches. At about that time Lyndon also spoke to Mrs Chapman, who said that her husband had been acting very strangely. Lyndon said that he had never been able to certify Chapman as insane because of lack of evidence. If he had known about the document and the will, and the telegram to the Petersfield postmaster, he would probably have certified him. (Ernest could therefore have saved Emily's life by consulting Lyndon.)

Mathews then asked Lyndon whether in his opinion Chapman was insane on the fateful morning. Lyndon replied that he had no doubt that he was not responsible for his actions and that he was absolutely insane at the time he committed the act. Lyndon was interrogated at some length by Mathews about the nature of insanity and whether insane people were capable of appreciating the difference between right and wrong and of realising the enormity of the crime they were committing. Lyndon was of the opinion that people could be insane and yet aware of what they were doing. A large number of insane people knew that they were doing wrong and yet were unable to prevent themselves from doing it, because they were subject to uncontrollable impulses, and that was what happened to Chapman. Dr Worthington, superintendent of the County Lunatic Asylum, said that he was convinced that Chapman was insane at the time of the attack and did not understand what he was doing. The Medical Officer of Winchester prison supported Worthington's opinion and agreed that Chapman acted under an impulse he could not control.

The judge in his summing up said that the jury would undoubtedly be of the opinion that the prisoner caused the death of his wife – the only question was whether he was responsible in law. All three medical men had come to the conclusion that Chapman was insane and not in control of his actions at the time. The jury consulted for only a minute or two. One of them asked whether there was any insanity in the prisoner's family. The judge said that was irrelevant. The jury then found the prisoner guilty but insane and not responsible in law. What else could they do when faced with all that medical evidence – blinded by science as we say now? The judge directed that Chapman should be detained in prison 'pending His Majesty's pleasure'. Chapman covered his face in his hands and was led from the dock. Before leaving the court he was allowed to speak to his brothers and his sister.

So ended the first Grayshott murder trial. Would Chapman have been declared insane today, a hundred years later? Perhaps, or perhaps not. Some people would say that a person should not be absolved from murder because of one or two cranky delusions, or because of a fit of uncontrollable temper. Wherever he finished up Chapman had plenty of time to reflect on his moment of madness.

'I HAVE JUST KILLED A MAN'

In October 1914 the first Canadian troops arrived in England to fight in the First World War. Many more followed in the next year or so as the war took its toll and casualties increased. On 3 December 1915 the Ninth Canadian Mounted Rifles under Lieutenant-Colonel Hodson came to Bramshott camp, where they joined the Forty-first Canadian Infantry Regiment, who had arrived several days earlier. Colonel Archambault of the Infantry Regiment had secured the use of a house named Arundel (now Hindhead Chase) in Crossways Road at Grayshott, a mile or two from the camp, for the use of himself, Major Hughes and Lieutenant Codere, the acting Adjutant. All three were expecting their wives to join them from Canada. The other officers resided at Bramshott camp, where they were now joined by the officers of the Mounted Rifles.

Colonel Hodson enquired of the other officers the best way of exchanging Canadian dollars into sterling, this money being the canteen takings on the voyage from Canada on the SS *California*. Lieutenant Codere immediately offered to exchange them, saying that he knew where to get the best exchange rate. Hodson therefore told his canteen sergeant, Henry Ozanne, to hand the money over to Codere – 1508 Canadian dollars. Ozanne was a native of Guernsey who had worked as a flour merchants' representative in London and Southampton before emigrating to Canada to take up farming. He was described by his officers as an intelligent and trustworthy man.

On Saturday 4 December Codere went to the Capital and Counties Bank at Bramshott and asked what rate they could offer for Canadian dollars. They quoted 4 dollars 85 cents to the pound. Codere seemed dissatisfied with that and did not exchange any dollars. He then cashed two cheques, for £60 and £90, promising that he would bring sufficient dollars on the Monday to refund his account. He did not return with the money as promised.

On the Monday Codere went to the foreign exchange department of Thomas Cook at Ludgate Circus in London and asked for 1735 Canadian dollars to be changed into sterling. He received £362, mostly in £5 notes. (Their rate was 4 dollars 80 cents to the pound.) By the following day his two cheques had been returned to the bank at Bramshott unpaid and were shown to Captain Morin of the Infantry Regiment. Morin found Codere and told him that he must repay the cheques immediately. Codere said that he would repay them presently. Morin insisted that they be repaid straight away so together they went to the bank and Codere gave Morin £150 to pay in to his (Codere's) account, for some reason not wanting to go into the bank himself.

On the afternoon of Wednesday 8 December Lance-Corporal Joseph Keller, Major Hughes's batman, was at Arundel when Codere and a soldier whom he did not recognize arrived by motor car and went into the parlour. He saw Codere fetch a bottle of whisky and two glasses from the kitchen. Keller went outside to feed the chickens and on return he met Codere in the kitchen. Said Codere, 'Don't talk, Joe. I have just killed a man.' He told Keller to fetch a bowl of water. Keller got the water and Codere told him to wash the blood off the floor of the parlour and along the passage leading to the cellar. Whatever Keller thought just then he kept to himself and did as he was told without comment. While Keller was cleaning the floor and Codere was inspecting the carpet Lance-Corporal Desjardins came in. 'Don't talk,' Codere said to him. 'I have just killed a man.' Desjardins at length said, 'Why did you do this, Mr Codere?' Codere replied, 'I killed him because I struck another man, and that man is the only one who saw me. That's why I killed him.' Codere took Keller and Desjardins to the cellar and said, 'Go and see him, he's there.' They went down a few steps and saw a body lying at the bottom. 'You are going to help me,' said Codere. Desjardins replied, No, Mr Codere, I cannot help you.' 'Then don't talk,' said Codere. 'Go to the grocer for steak and grapes.'

They all returned to the kitchen where Codere handed Keller a leather-covered lead stick, which had blood on one end. Keller recognized it as a stick that Codere sometimes carried in his pocket when it was not hanging up in the passage. 'Burn it,' he said. He told Keller to fetch two blankets and they went down to the cellar. Codere wrapped the body in the blankets. 'Help me to put him in the stable.' Each holding one end they carried the body to the stable, where Codere tied it round with wire. They returned to the house and Codere told Keller to remove his trousers, which were spotted with blood from the body. 'I will get you some clean ones. Wash this knife.' He handed Keller a knife covered in blood. They then returned to the stables to lock the doors. Later that evening Colonel Archambault and Major Hughes came in for supper and Codere joined them. Keller and Desjardins were too upset and frightened of Codere to say anything to the senior officers. At 10 pm Codere visited Sergeant Martin of the regimental transport and asked him to bring a large box to Arundel to put something in. Martin refused, saying that he could not take a transport wagon out at night without the permission of the Commanding Officer. His real reason for refusing was that he suspected Codere of joking, by asking him to fetch something that did not exist. He agreed to bring a box to Grayshott the following morning.

Early the next morning Keller reported the events of the previous afternoon to Major Hughes, who immediately woke Colonel Archambault. They found Codere at the officers' mess at Bramshott and Hughes arrested him. 'What for?' asked Codere. 'You know well,' replied Hughes. Meanwhile Sergeant Martin had arrived at Arundel with a large box in a wagon, which he parked near the stable. He met Keller and Desjardins, who told him the ghastly news, upon which he returned to Bramshott. Superintendent Reuben of the Hampshire Constabulary came to Bramshott later that day from Whitehill police station. He examined the dead body (which was that of Sergeant Ozanne) and charged Codere with his murder. Codere said he understood the charge and asked whether it would be a charge for the military or civil court. Reuben took him back to Whitehill, where Codere said that he could prove he was not the man in two minutes if they would give him the chance.

The inquest was held in the village hall on the following Monday. Evidence was given by Colonel Archambault, Colonel Hodson, Major Hughes, the other officers involved, and Corporals Keller and Desjardins. Dr Williams of Alton described the injuries to Ozanne. There were 45 wounds to the face and head, the neck was severed from ear to ear and the skull was fractured. All the wounds could have been caused by a knife and the skull was fractured by a blow. Codere declined to give evidence. After a brief retirement the coroner's jury returned a verdict of 'Guilty of murder'. Codere was committed for trial at the next Winchester assizes.

On Friday 4 February 1916 the trial began at Winchester of Lieutenant Georges Codere for the wilful murder of Sergeant Henry Ozanne. Two days previously an application for postponement of the case until the next assizes was made on behalf of Codere by his counsel. The main reason for wanting a postponement was to bring witnesses for the defence from Canada, some of whom would testify to there being insanity in Codere's family and indeed in Codere himself. The application was turned down by Mr Justice Darling. He said there was no certainty that these witnesses would come over from Canada. (They had already had two months to do so.) Also any or all of the witnesses at present stationed at Bramshott might be sent to France and be unavailable in six months time.

Counsel for the prosecution was Mr A.Clavell Salter and for the defence Mr J.A.Foote. Salter in his opening remarks described the events relating to the handing over to Codere of the Canadian dollars up to the time when Codere went to London to change them. Lieutenant Mercisse Morin, who had accompanied Codere to London, then gave evidence. He said that Codere showed him the dollars, saying that they belonged to someone in the Mounted Rifles. Codere asked Morin whether he wanted to make some money; he needed help 'to kill a man'. He said that he intended to get the receipt from the man in question and then knock him on the head with a trench stick, wrap the body in a blanket and then dispose of it (almost exactly what did happen later). Morin described Codere as a fool and said he was nicknamed 'Fou Codere' or 'Fool Codere' in the regiment. He could not be trusted to obey orders and was erratic in his behaviour.

After changing the money Codere went to the Savoy Hotel where he met another member of his regiment, Sergeant Martin. Martin in his evidence said that Codere had told him that he was going to kill a man by knocking him on the head and asked Martin whether he would help. He said that there was about 500 dollars in it and that Martin could have half. Martin was to come to Arundel at 10 am the following day and when he heard a yell he was to come in and hit a man on the head. Martin, who knew Codere well, assumed that he was joking and pretended to take him seriously. He told Codere that it would be better to poison the man and Codere asked him to recommend a good poison. He replied, 'Serum anti-tuberculeux,' and told Codere to use it in whisky, saying it would be effective within a second or two. Subsequently Codere attempted to buy some of this 'poison'. (It is not in fact a poison but an injection for the blood. So it had no effect when Ozanne drank the doctored whisky.)

Salter then described the events at Arundel prior to the murder, and the evidence of Keller and Desjardins relating to the discovery of the body. He produced a letter written by Codere (in French) to Keller, which in effect asked the latter to take the blame for the murder and he (Codere) would do his best to save him from punishment. Extracts from the letter read: 'Joe. I would keep my promise in taking all the means to save you, because I promised to help you, and I will do it. The thing has been discovered, and someone saw you strike him... The question of money is nothing. If it costs 5000 dollars or more I will pay them... As you have been seen to strike him, it is no use to put the thing on me, because I will not be able to help you if you put me in a hole... Having struck you, you wanted to take your revenge, and you struck him at a bad place. Seeing that you stunned him, you finished him... I helped you to hide him so as to get rid of him, but I did not do it, because someone told me that it was known. There is only one thing to do. That's to write on paper the truth: "I declare that it is myself who struck the sergeant who was found dead at Grayshott, and Lieut.Codere has nothing to do with it"... I will occupy myself with your defence.' Keller had been under arrest for a short while, because he had been suspected of the murder when his trousers were found beside the body (conveniently placed there by Codere!), but he was released when Codere became the obvious suspect.

Colonel Archambault described Codere's background and character. He said that Codere had been appointed assistant Adjutant (a post with no responsibilities) because he was of no use in any other position. He was useless for active service as he was not to be trusted with men's lives and would not have been sent to France. (How he passed the examination to qualify as an officer is a mystery.)

Witnesses were called by the prosecution and the defence to give their opinion of the mental state of the prisoner, the defence attempting to prove his insanity and the prosecution to deny it. Dr Thomas Stoddart, a defence witness and lecturer in mental diseases, thought that Codere was of unsound mind. His insanity rested on his inability to comprehend questions because he was incapable of paying attention to the speaker. Codere was convinced that he was the victim of a conspiracy. Dr Maurice Craig, a lecturer at Guy's Hospital, said that in his opinion Codere was not a normal person but he would not certify him as insane, even knowing the history of insanity in his family.

Foote, summing up for the defence, said the case hinged on the state of the prisoner's mind at the moment of the murder. Delusions and hallucinations did not prove insanity. If a person thought he was the Archbishop of Canterbury or that his head was made of glass he was deluded but not necessarily insane. On the other hand a person could be insane without any delusions. The jury had to consider the past history of the prisoner, the known insanity in his family, and his acts on the day of the crime. He suggested that the evidence showed that Codere was 'wrong in the head' even before the murder. He said that only an insane person would tell everybody that he was about to kill a person, and finished by asking the jury whether they could come to any other conclusion.

Salter, summing up for the prosecution, said the jury had to decide whether Codere knew that he was going to commit murder.

There was a motive for the crime – the money that he owed Ozanne. He had not intended to commit such a brutal crime, but when he found that the poison did not work he resorted to violence. Salter submitted that this was a premeditated murder committed for gain, the blame for which Codere had tried to put on Keller, and that far from being insane Codere had acted with malice aforethought.

The judge's summing up took one hour and twenty minutes. He said there was no question as to the identity of the murderer – it was obviously Codere. He said that insanity did not mean what many people and many doctors said it meant. It had been said by learned counsel that if they yielded to the argument that whoever committed a crime was insane, there was no point in holding assizes or having laws to punish crime, because all they would have to do would be to shut that person up in an asylum. Supposing they said that every man who committed a crime was under some degree of partial insanity, was a man who committed a crime and hid it, and did not get found out, any more insane than the man who committed a murder and did get found out? It was strange that if Codere had intended to commit a murder he should have talked about it, but apparently he was a foolish man. The mere fact that he had killed a man did not prove that he was mad. Did the prisoner know that it was wrong to beat a man's brains out and then cut his throat? If he did not know that it was wrong then he was insane. He had tried to hide the body – was that not evidence that he knew he had done wrong? The jury must decide whether in their opinion Codere at the moment of the crime did or did not know the seriousness of what he was doing. The jury retired for twenty minutes before returning a verdict of 'Guilty'. 'Guilty, simply?' asked Mr Justice Darling. 'Yes,' replied the foreman. Codere was sentenced to death by hanging.

The defence lodged an appeal, which was heard before the Lord Chief Justice. He said that Mr Justice Darling's summing up was unobjectionable and that the jury had reached a verdict after hearing all the evidence. He gave a learned explanation of the McNaghten rules relating to insanity as a defence in criminal trials, and dismissed the appeal. He added, however, that the Home Secretary had power to make further investigations, with regard to information that could not be available to the assize court or the appeal court. He was referring to the fact that Codere's family were under the impression that their evidence could be presented without their attendance at court. That was possible in Canadian courts but not in English courts.

Codere was not hanged. The Home Secretary exercised his discretion in favour of Codere and he was sent to a Canadian prison for

the insane. Was this a diplomatic decision made in order not to jeop-
ardize relations between Britain and Canada at this time? We shall
never know. The curious fact remains that the verdicts in the two
murder cases at Grayshott both depended on the defence of insanity.
In the Chapman case it was a straightforward decision by the trial
jury. In the Codere case it had to be referred to the Lord Chief Justice
and the Home Secretary for a final decision.

KILLER ON THE RUN

In the early morning of Sunday 25 April 1920 a farm labourer named Burridge was cycling along the Amesbury to Andover road (numbered A303 when numbering was introduced). In those days it was quite safe to cycle along main roads. He was near the village of Thruxton when he saw a man lying on the ground behind a hedge. He thought the man was probably a tramp, as tramps were a common sight then with ex-servicemen returning from the war unable to find employment or claim benefits. On second thoughts he decided to have a closer look, and was horrified to find that the man was covered in blood and unquestionably dead.

Burridge cycled quickly into the village and informed the police. When the man was examined he was found to be Sidney Spicer, a twenty-nine-year-old married taxi-driver from Salisbury. He had last been seen in Salisbury at about 9 pm the previous evening, when his cab was hired by two men, two women and a soldier to take them to Bulford army camp. Spicer had been shot in the head and robbed and his body partly concealed by dragging it across the road face down, over a bank and through the hedge, into a shallow hole in the ground where gamekeepers had been digging for rabbits. His face had therefore been lacerated and made almost unrecognizable. There would not have been much traffic in 1920 late on a Saturday evening, even on a main road, to disturb the killer.

But what was Spicer doing at Thruxton, which is some 7 or 8 miles off the route from Salisbury to Bulford? He might have picked up another passenger at Bulford Camp who had asked to be taken to Thruxton. He was thought to have had about £20 on him at the time of the attack, but this money, his driver's licence and other articles were missing, as indeed was his taxi-cab. Spicer had once had his own taxi, before joining the Army. He had been employed as a taxi-driver for the last two weeks by the owner of the cab, and most of his journeys were between Salisbury and Bulford with soldiers. The official description of the missing car makes interesting reading eighty years later:

'No. AM 2290. 12 horsepower Darracq of 1912 pattern. The registration number is painted on the radiator. The body of the car is painted french grey, and the upholstery is in black leather. The car is a five-seater. It has an Overland dynamo, fitted with ordinary bicycle free-wheel and ordinary bicycle chain, black leather universal joints, Bennett carburettor, Bosch magneto and a home-made switchboard. Riley's wired wheels, black sheet-iron pins, two Ford head-lamps, electric rear lamp and two Lucas black side lamps. Bates retread tyre on near hind wheel, Michelin square tread back offside wheel, Bates retread tyre near side front wheel and Michelin on front offside wheel. Bates retread spare wheel. The bed spring near offside has been recently repaired. The value of the car is £350.'

The car was found on the Monday evening in a suburb of Swansea, and had been deliberately made unroadworthy with the magneto wire cut and the wheels damaged. The finding of the car did not help in the identification of the murderer, but an important clue was given by one of the passengers on that last trip to Bulford. This witness said that Spicer had stopped at Amesbury to look at his petrol gauge. While doing so a man asked him for a lift to Andover. Spicer said that when he had dropped his passengers he would return and take the man to Andover. The man was described as tall and in sergeant-major's uniform. At Bulford Spicer bought some petrol in a two-gallon can. Further enquiries by the police revealed that a grey Darracq had stopped at a Cirencester garage at 8 am on the Sunday for repairs. It left two hours later and stopped again at Gloucester for petrol. There were two men in the car, both in uni-form, and they arrived at Swansea on Sunday evening and spent the night at the Grosvenor Hotel. The following descriptions of the men were issued:

1. Age from 35 to 40; height 5ft. 8in. or 9in., medium build; dressed in khaki trousers and British warm; wearing gold crown denoting rank of company sergeant-major.

2. Age 19-21; height 5ft. 6in.; clean-shaven; full face; wearing glasses; bearing the letters ASC on shoulder-straps; also in khaki.

Using that second description the police soon arrested one of the men, a private in the Royal Army Service Corps at Bulford Camp. The arrest followed a parade of all the units on Salisbury Plain when the soldier was identified. As a result of his information the police then issued a further description of the second man as follows:

'Private Percy Toplis, Number E.M.T. 54262 M.T., RASC, of Bulford Camp. Joined the RASC in August and was reported a deserter in December. Aged thirty-four. Height 5ft. 8in. or 5ft. 9in. Medium build. Fair complexion, slight fair ginger moustache. Fair eyebrows and hair. Smart appearance. Had posed as an officer of the Royal Air Force, and is believed to be a deserter from the RAF. Was in possession of a Mark VI Webley revolver.'

He was said to be wearing a blue suit, a fawn soft felt hat, and also a gold-rimmed monocle. The police warned that he was likely to use the revolver if necessary. This description initiated a police hunt over the whole country, and the residents of Swansea in particular conducted a thorough search of their area. On the Monday night farmers, labourers and miners combed the district by moonlight but without success. The private who was arrested at Bulford said that he was not with Toplis at the time of the murder but met him on the road to Swansea and stayed the night there with him.

The inquest on Spicer was opened at Thruxton Farm that week. The coroner said that the circumstances pointed strongly to murder. Only three witnesses were called. Tom Spicer said that his brother was a 'happy-go-lucky' man with no enemies; he had last seen him that same Saturday morning. George Heather of Bulford said that he saw Spicer dropping passengers at the camp and Spicer remarked that he was short of petrol as he had to go to Andover. Heather gave him a tin of petrol. Dr Farr, the police surgeon, said that there were bruises on the body that might have been caused by being dragged across the road, obviously by quite a strong man. There were scratches on the left cheek, bruises on the head and nose and a round wound on the scalp half an inch wide. At the post-mortem he had discovered a bullet embedded in the brain. From its position he deduced that it had been fired from behind the victim and from the left side. The wound could not have been self-inflicted. The inquest was then adjourned for a fortnight.

Meanwhile other facts relating to Toplis came to light. He was it seems audacious to the point of foolhardiness and made little attempt to hide his intentions or after the murder his whereabouts. On the Saturday morning of the crime he had shown his revolver to a friend in Southampton, saying that he was going to make some use of it. In the evening, soon after the murder, he called at Bulford Camp for Private Henry Fallows, the man currently under arrest, and they had supper with the mess cook before departing for Swansea. From Swansea he went to London and wrote a letter to Fallows that was intercepted by the police. Toplis was apparently known in many parts of the country.

Toplis had been declared a deserter from the RASC on 26 December 1919. He joined the RAF as a No. 2 air mechanic and was posted to Uxbridge, from where he again deserted in March. When he absconded from the RASC at Bulford Camp a Sunbeam touring car, worth £1,000, also disappeared. Despite the danger of being arrested for desertion at any time he had apparently slept at Bulford Camp for several nights just before the murder. All of which of course does not say very much for military efficiency and security in the

1920s. It was said that he had many different identities and aliases and was often seen as a lieutenant-colonel. He carried a brown case with him in which were his disguises. His manner was decribed as aristocratic and he was adept at acquiring money. His mother stated that he enlisted in the RAMC in 1914, left in 1918 and rejoined the Army in 1919.

After their night at Swansea Toplis and Fallows left the car and boarded a train, Toplis going to London and Fallows to Salisbury on his way back to Bulford. When Fallows arrived back at camp he was given seven days 'confined to barracks' for being absent and his arrest followed. He said that Toplis asked him to go with him to Swansea and promised to pay his return fare. (He met Toplis at Bulford on the Saturday evening, not on the road to Swansea.) Meanwhile the police were searching for Toplis in London, and a visit to the Union Jack Club drew a blank. They were said to be in possession of 'correspondence of an important nature'.

When the inquest was resumed at Andover a verdict of wilful murder was given against Toplis, who had still not been found. Most of the evidence was supplied by Fallows, but before he gave it Private Holdrick of the Southampton Embarkation Depot told of his meeting with Toplis on the Saturday morning. Toplis said that he was in the RAF, having obtained his ticket from the OSC. He told Holdrick that he had taken the missing Sunbeam car from Bulford and sold it for £400. He said that he was going to Bulford to get another car and that if he could not get it by fair means he would get it with the revolver, which he showed to Holdrick.

Fallows said that Toplis had promised him a ride in a motor car and he finally turned up at 11 pm at the cookhouse asking for a drink. He said, 'If you don't go for your ride now I shan't be able to take you, as I have some business on.' At North Tidworth Toplis asked a policeman for some water (for himself or the car?). For part of the journey Toplis wore his crown on his coat, and at other times took it off. Fallows asked Toplis what the loaded revolver was for. He replied, 'If anybody gets in my way I will do them in.' In Savernake Forest Toplis got out and burnt some clothes; he told Fallows that they were useless rags. Throughout the journey Toplis rarely spoke and seemed nervous and worried. They reached Swansea at 6.45 pm on the Sunday. (A 1912 Darracq was not capable of high speeds, even although there could not have been much traffic.)

They stayed at the Grosvenor Hotel but understandably overslept, after missing a night's sleep. After breakfast they started off again in the car, but on spotting a policeman Toplis turned abruptly into another street. In this street they saw another policeman and Toplis asked, 'Is he looking?' He then told Fallows to get out, borrowed his spectacles, and drove off. He came back in ten minutes without the car, saying someone else had got it. He was obviously getting worried that a policeman would recognize it from the circulated description. He gave Fallows £1 for his fare to Bulford as they walked to the station. Every time they saw a policeman Toplis hid behind Fallows, asking, 'Is he looking?' On being asked why he was so afraid of the police, Toplis replied, 'So would you be if you'd had as much to do with them as I have.' When they parted at Salisbury Toplis promised to write to Fallows or come to see him. Fallows said that Toplis never went on parade, was absent from Thursday of one week to Wednesday of the next, and wrote his own leave warrants. (Army discipline in the 1920s was obviously a bit slack to say the least.)

Fallows was later charged with receiving, harbouring and maintaining Percy Toplis in the knowledge that Toplis had committed murder. Fallows himself made no statement, but what he said to the police at the time was given as evidence. He had said that he knew nothing of the murder until he read it in the newspapers. The funeral of Sidney Spicer was attended by a large number of people, among them many licensed taxi-drivers, who laid a wreath in the shape of a motor wheel.

The quest for Toplis went on until the afternoon of Sunday 6 June. At the village of High Hesket on the main road between Carlisle and Penrith Police Constable Alfred Fulton saw a soldier sitting near a dike. The soldier got up and walked away when Fulton approached, throwing his kitbag over his shoulder. On being questioned the soldier said that he was on his way to Penrith. He produced a duty ticket from Aberdeen and explained that he was on escort duty. Fulton told him that if he was on escort duty he would have been on a train. The soldier then admitted that he was an absentee, so Fulton let him go on his way but hurried home. There he looked at the description of the wanted Toplis and realised that he had just been speaking to him.

He returned to the village on his bicycle and eventually found the man in a plantation. He said, 'Hello, boy, is this as far as you have got?' The soldier got to his feet and pulled out a revolver, shouting, 'Hands up.' Fulton did as he was told. 'It is me you are looking for, is it?' asked the soldier. 'If you are, I am Toplis. I shot the policeman and the farmer and if you act the same, you go too.' (He had attempted to murder a policeman and a farmer in Banffshire the previous week.) He made Fulton drop his handcuffs and truncheon on the ground and then lowered his revolver. Fulton told him to get out of the district and Toplis replied, 'I will kill or be killed.' Toplis then made his getaway, changing into civilian clothes from his kitbag before doing so.

Fulton hurried home, changed into civilian clothes because he knew that he would have to pass Toplis on the way and did not want to be recognized, borrowed a motor-cycle and sped to Penrith police station. Inspector Ritchie, Sergeant Bertram and Fulton were immediately sent back to High Hesket in a motor car, armed on the authority of the Chief Constable with revolvers. When they reached Plumpton they passed Toplis so turned round and passed him from the other direction. Ritchie ordered the driver to go on until they were out of sight, then they stopped and hid behind a wall. When Toplis reached them Ritchie stepped out and shouted, 'Stop!' Toplis started to run and turning round as he ran fired twice at the police from a distance of 5 yards. He was about to fire for a third time when Ritchie and Bertram shot him through the heart and he fell into Ritchie's arms. Both his shots had narrowly missed Ritchie, and both the policemen would surely have been killed had they not been armed.

The inquest on Toplis was held at Penrith town hall. He was identified by a private from Bulford Camp. An interesting diary was found in Toplis's possession, which related his movements since the beginning of the year. He mentioned visits to Bristol, Cardiff, Swansea, London, Swansea again (robbery), Bristol again (bought monocle), Bath, Chepstow, Salisbury, Southampton, Winchester, Freshford and Bulford, and concluded, 'Hunting West Wales; some hopes.' The jury returned a verdict of justifiable homicide and said that the police acted with discretion and care. They congratulated the police officers on their intelligence and 'promptitude'.

In spite of the fact that the police officers would have been killed had they not carried arms there must have been questions raised in Parliament about the affair, because the editor of the *Southern Daily Echo* saw fit to criticize the 'milk-and-water theorists of Westminster', saying that he preferred the life of one Constable Fulton to the lives of half a dozen Toplises. The *Yorkshire Evening Post* said that although it was not desirable to arm every village policeman, in cases like this it would have been folly to send unarmed officers to deal with a desperate criminal. With which sentiments all reasonable people must agree, even if there are 'theorists' today who think otherwise.

'POOR FRED IS DEAD. HE MUST HAVE HAD A FIT'

The village of Lower Wield lies in a remote part of the county, about 8 miles south of Basingstoke and 6 miles west of Alton, and is reached by quiet country roads from the neighbouring villages of Upper Wield, Bradley and Bentworth. There is a public house, the Yew Tree, but no shops. In 1920 it was even quieter; the nearest railway station was at Medstead on what is now the Watercress Line. At Nicholas's Farm (now Nicholas Farm) lived Mrs Fanny Messenger and her six children, four boys and two girls, Philip the eldest boy being her son from her first marriage. Her second husband had died in 1919 and she carried on the business of the farm with the help of her children.

On Saturday 8 May 1920 Norman Messenger, eighteen-years-old and the second eldest of the children, ate his lunch by himself and left the house at 1.45 pm to visit the Windmill public house. His two sisters had left the house a short time previously. He did not see his mother or his two younger brothers, Fred aged seventeen and Reginald aged twelve, but he suspected they were somewhere in the house or garden. Fred had been a cripple since birth and could walk only with difficulty. Norman was at the Windmill for half an hour then went to the cricket-field, where he saw his half-brother Philip Westbrook playing cricket. He wandered around the village and into the cricket-field, until Reginald brought him a message from his mother to return home.

When he arrived home he found his mother and Philip in the kitchen bending over the body of his brother Fred. His mother looked up and said, 'Here's poor Fred.' It was clear to Norman that his brother was dead. His mother said that he had had a fit and told Norman to send for a policeman or a doctor. He went to Bentworth, 2 miles away, and told Police Constable Hill what had happened. 'My young brother has dropped dead.' Hill cycled to Lower Wield and met Mrs Messenger. 'Fred has just had a fit and broke a blood vessel and died,' she said. 'I have sent for Dr Hodgson at Alton.' Hill found the boy lying on his back in a pool of blood, with his arms stretched out. He noticed a large wound under the right eye.

When Dr Hodgson arrived he looked at the wound and said, 'He has been shot with a shot-gun.' While the doctor was examining the body Constable Hill noticed two shot-guns hanging on a kitchen beam. He took one down and found that the left-hand barrel had been used recently as it smelled of gunpowder and looked dirty. Philip said that it was his gun and he had last used it on the Tuesday of that week. Hill asked Dr Hodgson to telephone Superintendent Reuben at Whitehill. For the next twenty minutes Hill searched the room in vain for the empty cartridge case. Mrs Messenger then came in to lay the table for tea. Hill watched as she bent down between the wall and the piano and to his astonishment picked up a cartridge case. ' It was not there just now,' he said. 'I have just searched the floor.' He felt sure it was not there when he had searched the floor. To his further astonishment the family then came in and proceeded to have their tea with the body lying there, as if nothing had happened.

When Superintendent Reuben arrived Hill showed him the gun and the cartridge case and Reuben agreed that the gun had been used recently. He asked Mrs Messenger to account for the boy's death. 'He has had a fit,' she said, 'and broke a blood vessel. Dr Hodgson told me that he would have another and then die.' 'How do you account for the hole in his face?' asked Reuben. 'That is where he knocked himself about,' she replied. 'They do when they have a fit.' 'He has not had a fit,' said Reuben. 'He has been shot.' Mrs Messenger said that the doctor had made a mistake. She added that Fred had been a great trial to her, for it took all her time to look after him. Reuben then asked Philip when he had last used the gun. Philip replied, 'On the Thursday evening last.' (He had told Constable Hill that he had last used it on the Tuesday.)

The inquest opened on 11 May but was adjourned until 27 May. On 14 May the story took a dramatic turn when Reuben went to Nicholas's Farm and charged Mrs Messenger and Philip with feloniously killing Fred Messenger with a gun. 'I am innocent,' said Mrs Messenger. 'So am I,' said Philip. They were remanded to Winchester prison by the Alton magistrates.

The inquest was held at Nicholas's Farm, outside on the lawn as it was a fine day. The first witness, Norman Messenger, said that his brothers were on good terms with each other, and that Fred was not a great deal of trouble. He confirmed that when he left to go to the Windmill he had not seen anyone else in the house. Philip Westbrook in his evidence said that he last saw Fred alive at about 10 am. When he went out after lunch his mother was in the house but he saw none of his brothers. When he arrived home after being called from the cricket-field he found his mother, who was crying, and the baker in the kitchen with the dead boy. He said now that he had last used the gun on the Monday or Tuesday and had left the barrel dirty.

He had never heard anyone threaten Fred.

Mrs Messenger said that Fred had always been a cripple and that he was unable to use his hands very well, his left hand not at all. It would have been quite impossible for him to have loaded and fired a gun. She last saw Fred alive in his grandmother's garden, about 80 yards away, between 2 and 3 pm playing with Reginald. She went to her allotment at 2.45 pm for half an hour. Philip had already left the house on his bicycle. On the way back she met the baker, who accompanied her to the house. When she found Fred she thought that he had had a fit and injured his head on the floor. She had no idea that he had been shot until Dr Hodgson told her so. She said the only person she employed was a carter, who she presumed was out in the fields with his horses at the time of the shooting.

Reginald Messenger said that his mother spoke to him and Fred while they were in his grandmother's garden. Fred said he was going home to clean out the stable and Reginald stayed at his grandmother's. He saw his mother and the baker walking towards the house and followed them. He went into the kitchen and saw Fred, and his mother told him to fetch his brothers from the cricket-field. Eric Bowman, the baker, said that he arrived at Nicholas's Farm at 3.30 pm, met Mrs Messenger in the road and accompanied her to the front door, which opened on to a short passage. As she stepped inside the kitchen she said, 'Poor Fred is dead. He must have had a fit.'

Dr Hodgson then gave his evidence relating to the injury. He said that the gun-shot wound was almost horizontal in direction, indicating that the shot was fired from a height of 4 feet 6 inches above the floor, about the height a normal adult would have held the gun, and about 3 feet away from the victim. The boy had staggered backwards two steps, fallen on his back and bled to death. Whoever had fired the shot took out the cartridge and replaced the gun on the beam. Fred could not possibly have shot himself and replaced the gun. He said that the left-hand barrel had been used recently, and the powder smelled quite fresh. He had later conducted an experiment by firing a cartridge from a gun and then smelling the barrel at intervals, and had found that the fresh smell of the powder disappeared after about twelve hours.

Superintendent Reuben related his conversation with Mrs Messenger regarding the cause of death, and what he knew of the movements of the members of the family that afternoon. He added the additional information that Philip had returned from the Windmill briefly at about 2.30 pm to fetch two rabbits for the landlady of the inn, and that when he left only his mother was in the house.

The coroner told the jury that there could be no doubt as to the cause of death and the real question for them to determine was whether the boy had inflicted the wound on himself or whether some other person had done so wilfully or accidentally. They had heard evidence that it would have been impossible for him to have shot himself. Two people had been arrested and charged with the murder and if the jury thought that there was sufficient evidence to show that these two people were responsible they must say so. No suggestion had been made that they had been cleaning the gun and that it been discharged accidentally. If the jury were of the opinion that some unknown person had entered the house, taken down the gun and shot the boy, then they must say so. The jury consulted for five minutes and the foreman said, 'We find that the deceased was shot by some person unknown.' The coroner said, 'You mean that some person or persons unknown wilfully and deliberately murdered him. Is that what you mean?' 'Yes, sir,' said the foreman.

Mrs Messenger and Philip were charged at Alton magistrates court with the murder of Fred Messenger. Mr Harold Murphy outlined the case for the prosecution. He suggested that the murder had occurred at 2.45 pm, at about the time when Philip had returned to the farm to fetch the rabbits. He said it was pure imagination on the part of Mrs Messenger to say that the boy had had a fit. She did not seem surprised or horrified at the discovery, and later they had all sat down to tea in the presence of the body, indicating an absence of natural affection. She must have been at the farm when the shot was fired. It went against all the evidence and all reason to assume that some unknown person had entered the house, found the cartridges in a place where no stranger would have known where to look, and killed the boy.

The witnesses repeated the evidence they had given at the inquest. Mrs Messenger explained that when she had said previously that Fred was a 'great trial' she had meant only that he was a trouble to keep clean. She could have put him in a home years ago had she wished. When she found his body she thought he must have had a fit because she could not believe that anybody would have shot him. Philip and his mother denied all knowledge of the crime. They were committed for trial at the next Winchester assizes.

Another dramatic turn of events unfolded at the trial. It began when Ernest Charles, the prosecuting counsel, addressed the crowded court. He said that after reading all the witnesses' statements he would not be justified in accepting the verdict of the jury on the existing evidence. It had been brought to his notice that the young brother of the deceased (Reginald) had made a confession, in which he stated that he had shot his brother by accident when playing with a loaded gun. He thought that this served to corroborate the conclusion to which he had already come. He asked Mr Emanuel, the defence counsel, to hand the confession to the judge, Mr Justice Bray. The judge asked Charles to read it out to the court. This confession, dated 28 June, is worth quoting in full and comparing with the evidence of the witnesses:

'The statement contained in my deposition, taken before the Alton justices, is true as far as the words "That happened before Fred and I went to get the water." I wish now to alter what I said subsequently, and make the following statement of my own free will. After my mother had gone up the lane, Fred and I both went back to Nicholas's Farm together. We both went in by the front door. Fred went in first and I followed. The kitchen door was shut, and Fred opened [it] and went in, and stood by the window looking out of it. I got on to a chair by the end of the table, and took down Philip's gun. I undid the strap on which it hung nearest the door. I took the gun down to clean it, and put it on the round table in the window while I looked for the cleaner. I could not find the cleaner. The gun was pointing towards Fred, who was still looking out of the window, and I picked it up to hang it up again, when it went off straight at Fred's face. Fred fell over, and I took out the cartridge case, and threw it on the floor by the piano. I hung the gun up again. I was very frightened, and ran out of the front door, which I shut. I ran off up the back of my grandmother's garden, in the back way, and looked out of the front window. I saw the baker, and came out of my grandmother's cottage. The baker spoke to me, and I looked up the road, and saw my mother by Smith's cottage, and called to her. I then went down to the farm behind my mother and the baker. I have never told this before, because I was afraid. I told my uncle yesterday.'

Mr Charles declared that he would offer no evidence. Mr Emanuel said that the boy had confessed to his uncle, who told him that he was not satisfied with it, and they must go to the house so that he could demonstrate just how the accident had occurred. In the kitchen Reginald stood on a chair, took down the gun and showed his uncle how it went off accidentally. The uncle decided to send the statement to the Public Prosecutor. Emanuel said that in the circumstances he was not surprised by the decision of Mr Charles not to offer any evidence and he asked the judge therefore not to proceed with the trial.

The judge immediately instructed the jury to return a verdict of 'Not Guilty'. He said he could not recollect any case in which an instance of this sort had occurred. It would have been a farce to proceed with the trial and conclude with the confession. He had read through the evidence several times and had come to the conclusion that there was no evidence on which the prisoners could have been convicted. He said that if there had been a grand jury the prisoners would never have been put on trial. To his regret grand juries had been dispensed with and he looked forward to the time when they would be restored. He had no doubt as to the truth of the confession, even although the boy had not disclosed the truth before the magistrates. He was glad to find the case ending in the way that he had anticipated. The jury duly returned a verdict of 'Not Guilty'. The confession seemed to come as a great relief to the judge and the two learned counsels, for presumably it saved them from a long deliberation over a great deal of conflicting evidence.

So the case ended apparently to everyone's satisfaction. But many questions remained unresolved, indeed not even mentioned at the inquest or at the trial. Why did Reginald wait such a long time (from 14 May to 28 June) before making his confession? Even at the tender age of twelve he must have known or been told why his mother and brother were in prison and that if found guilty they would be executed. Was he so frightened of the consequences of confessing? But perhaps nobody had the courage to tell him what a serious position they were in.

Who loaded the gun? Philip said that he fired the left-hand barrel a few days before the accident and put the gun away without cleaning it; he did not say whether or not he reloaded it. Reginald in his confession said nothing about loading the gun, only that the gun went off as he was putting it away. The evidence of the police officers had established that the same barrel was used. He must have assumed that the gun was empty or he would not have attempted to clean it. In any case he would have had no reason to load it. Why did he take it into his head to clean the gun? Was he in the habit of cleaning the gun? If it went off accidentally it would seem long odds against the gun being pointed in the exact direction of Fred's face. Why did he not run for help? He did not run away immediately but according to his statement stopped to remove the cartridge and replace the gun on the beam.

Why was Mrs Messenger so unconcerned about Fred's death? Did she really believe that he had had a fit? How did she find a cartridge case when Constable Hill had already made an extensive search for it? All in all we would have to agree with the judge and the counsels that the evidence was inconclusive. Perhaps Sherlock Holmes would have solved it.

MURDER IN BLOSSOM ALLEY

On Saturday 27 January 1923 as Mary Riley walked past the house of her neighbour Mary Pelham in Blossom Alley, a narrow passage between North Street and Cross Street not far from Portsmouth docks, she noticed that the door was ajar and the shutters still closed, even although it was 1.15 pm. She put her head round the door and called Mary's name, but getting no answer climbed the stairs to the bedroom. There a shocking sight greeted her – Mary Pelham was lying on the bed soaked in blood, with her head and face battered in. Almost falling down the stairs in her hurry, Mary Riley ran to Queen Street and told a police constable what she had found. He informed two other officers, who went to Blossom Alley and looked at the body but wisely did nothing until the arrival of Detective-Inspector Penford.

Near the body was a broken bottle covered in blood, which was probably what had been used to kill her. The injuries to the head had been made with great force. 'He must have acted like a maniac,' said one of the officers. Round her neck was a scarf or piece of ribbon, suggesting that the killer had tried to strangle her before hitting her. The bed and the floor were covered in blood. Mary Pelham had been living for about four years in this house, which consisted of three rooms one above the other and was poorly furnished. This neighbourhood in 1923 was a slum area of the worst kind, unhealthy and of bad reputation. Mary Pelham was known to be a prostitute and took sailors home with her most evenings. On that particular evening she had been seen returning between 10.30 and 11 pm with a man. It was strange that neither the woman who lived opposite her across the narrow alley, who was an insomniac, nor the woman who slept in the adjoining house separated by only a thin wall, heard any noise that night.

There being no obvious clues to pursue it was decided to call on the services of Chief Detective Inspector Mercer of Scotland Yard. He first of all tried to trace Mary's movements on the fateful evening. She had been to a small café in Queen Street at about 10.30 pm to get some 'mash for the kitten' and some 'chips for my man at home'. No-one was with her at that time. Prior to this she had been seen with a sailor in an Italian restaurant. This sailor was soon traced to HMS *Ramillies* and was interviewed by the police, as a result of which he was for the time being refused permission to leave the ship. Meanwhile the bottle found in the bedroom was sent to Scotland Yard for fingerprinting.

Although the murderer was thought likely to be a sailor, the possibility of a civilian being involved was not discounted. The scarf round the woman's neck was of the type often worn by working men as well as women, and was tied with a granny knot, which a sailor would not have used. Her remark in the café about a 'man at home' suggested that she had a civilian waiting for her rather than a sailor. The next lead came from Horndean, on the road to Petersfield. A stranger had entered the Brewers Arms on Saturday evening and ordered a glass of beer, then began reading the *Evening News* on the counter. When he came to the late news column, which had a brief reference to the murder, he was observed to become quite agitated. 'He could not keep still,' said the landlady. He kept looking round as if expecting someone. On being asked why he was so upset he said that he had witnessed a tragedy in Charlotte Street, Portsmouth, that day and could not forget it, but did not give any more details. He was wearing ill-fitting civilian clothes. As he left he said that he was going for a bus to Petersfield. He was next seen in the Ship and Bell public house, still agitated. The landlord described him as about thirty years old, with tattoo marks on one arm. The man said he was a deserter, accounting for his nervousness. He left very soon and was never seen again, either in Horndean or Petersfield. It was a pity that the police never tried to find him, for he was a promising suspect.

On the Monday another stranger was seen in Horndean on his way to Petersfield. He gave some villagers a detailed description of the Portsea murder and said that he had been detained at Portsmouth police station in connection with it, then released on giving a suitable alibi. The police later denied interviewing anyone of his description. Perhaps the residents of Horndean were getting suspicious of all strangers, especially those who made up fanciful stories about the murder.

The intense local interest in the crime turned to farce on the Wednesday when a large crowd assembled near Blossom Alley to await a pack of bloodhounds that it was rumoured were to be put on the trail of the killer. This absurd idea was no more than a rumour. It was now thought that the killer was more likely to have been a civilian, even possibly a woman intent on robbery or revenge. No jewellery or money was found in the house, and neighbours said that Mary Pelham was particularly hard up at the time, so if robbery was the motive the murderer was unlucky.

On the Wednesday evening an extraordinary event took place at the Royal Naval Barracks. Inspector Mercer went there with those women who had claimed to have seen Mary with a sailor on the evening of the murder. An identity parade of some of the sailors was organized, but it was found that one man who was particularly sought was not among those on parade. In consequence every man at the barracks was called out, all 3500 of them, in front of the women, forming perhaps the largest identity parade in the history of crime. One of the women picked out a certain sailor who she said had been with Mary that evening. It so happened that he was the man who had dodged the first identity parade. He was taken away by the police but nothing further was reported, so obviously he gave a satisfactory explanation.

The inquest opened on the Thursday following the murder. The coroner outlined the facts of the case and called witnesses. The first was the dead woman's husband, who lived at Shoreham, Sussex. He said that he had lived apart from his wife for some time and had last seen her about three or four years ago. She was thirty-seven years old. He knew that she was living as a prostitute. When he had seen her for the last time she had taken him to her house in Blossom Alley, but he had been so appalled by the filth and squalor that he left immediately and never saw her again.

Mary Riley said that she had been quite friendly with Mary Pelham, who was in the habit of visiting her every morning for a cup of tea. She last saw her alive at about 7 pm on the Friday. She related the details of what she found when she went upstairs to the bedroom. She had not seen anyone with Mary that evening. No-one to her knowledge had ever threatened her, nor was she on bad terms with anyone.

Police Constable Sheppard gave evidence of what he found when he went to Blossom Alley. He said that Mrs Pelham was lying on her shoulder and right hip, with a large wound on the forehead extending to the top of the nose. Her face was covered in blood, her tongue was protruding and round her neck was a light blue scarf; on the floor were two pools of blood. There was a lamp burning in the room. Asked about a ticket found on the bedside table, he said it was a ticket for a bedroom at the Royal Sailors' Rest (a hostel where sailors slept overnight). It was dated 15 January (nearly two weeks before the murder). There was no name on the ticket and no further information was obtained from the hostel because the names of men who slept there were not recorded.

Detective Inspector Penford spoke of his visit to Blossom Alley after being informed of the murder. He said that Mrs Pelham's house was part of a building containing 12 rooms, let to four different people. The furniture in the bedroom, which was dirty, consisted of two tables, a chair, a wash-stand and a double bed. The coroner asked him whether the house was fit for habitation. Penford could have replied that it depended on the class of person living there, but instead he said that the living conditions were very bad. 'Should it be condemned?' asked the coroner. Penford thought that it should, because two houses in the alley fell down only twelve months previously. He said that the alley did not give so much trouble to the police now that alcohol was more expensive. 'Is this some of the worst property in Portsmouth?' asked the coroner. 'Yes,' said Penford. 'I can't say that I know of any worse.'

Police Constable Young said that he saw Mrs Pelham at 10.30 pm in North Street with a sailor walking towards Blossom Alley. Fifteen minutes later he saw her enter the café in Queen Street with a basin, and that was the last he saw of her. He could not describe the sailor. The inquest was adjourned then to a later date in case evidence came to light that would lead to the capture of the murderer. It never did. Three weeks after arriving in Portsmouth Chief Detective Inspector Mercer returned to London leaving the case in the hands of the baffled local police force. The murderer was never found. The nearest the police came to solving the case was when Scotland Yard officers went to a house in London where a Navy reservist lodged. Unfortunately he was on a ship bound for South America. When the officers examined a trunk of clothes at the house they found a sailor's suit with bloodstains on one sleeve.

The notoriety of this case at least had one effect. It revealed to the upper-class and middle-class residents of this part of the county exactly what conditions were like in the lower-class slum areas. Never going anywhere near those areas of course they would have had no idea. A few years later the courts and alleys near Queen Street, including Blossom Alley, were demolished in the course of redevelopment and rehousing the inhabitants.

THE SOUTHAMPTON GARAGE MURDER

On Thursday 10 January 1929 Henry Passmore was in a good humour as he walked along Grove Street in Southampton. He had just been appointed as the local representative of the Wolf's Head Oil Company and with unemployment rising he was pleased to have a job. He was on his way to the garage at No. 42 where his predecessor, Vivian Messiter, had kept his motor car and his stock of lubricating oil. He wondered what had become of Messiter, who had not been seen or heard of since he left his lodgings on 30 October last year. Perhaps he had left the country for a while – he had travelled a good deal abroad and it was said that he had been divorced some years ago. The company had written to Messiter several times, but getting no reply had decided to appoint another representative.

Passmore found the garage doors padlocked but with the help of a neighbour forced them open. Inside he found Messiter's motor car and a large number of boxes containing cans of oil. He tried to start the car but found that the petrol tank was empty. He started to examine the stock of oil and then stumbled over a body – the body of a dead man, who was lying on his back, his face eaten away by rats and unrecognizable. When Passmore had got over the shock of his discovery he hurried out to call the police.

The body was identified at the mortuary as Messiter by Albert Parrott, his landlord, who recognized his clothes, his shoes and the colour of his hair. Soon after Messiter had disappeared Parrott had gone to the garage in Grove Street. Finding the outer doors locked he had climbed over a wall into the yard of the premises and found that the garage doors were padlocked. Parrott assumed that Messiter had gone away, perhaps even to the USA, for some undisclosed reason, but wondered why he had not been told. He had already informed the police that Messiter was missing and they issued a description of the missing man. A sergeant went to Grove Street, but finding the garage locked came away and left it at that. Messiter was a man of regular habits but had no known friends so his disappearance was not followed up. He had been a captain in the Canadian Army in the First World War. A strange fact came to light later – Southampton Chamber of Commerce had elected him a member while he was lying dead in the garage.

The Southampton police were confronted with a first-class mystery. Messiter had evidently been murdered but how and by whom was not at all clear. As ten weeks had elapsed since Messiter's death they decided to call in Scotland Yard and so Chief Inspector Prothero, one of their most experienced officers, was sent to investigate. *The Times*, whose headlines on the Saturday read 'MAN SHOT IN A GARAGE : SUSPECTED MURDER AT SOUTHAMPTON', reported that a post-mortem examination had revealed a bullet wound in the head. On the following Monday *The Times* again referred to a shot in the head, the theory then held by the police.

Even when a hammer was found in the garage the police did not discard the bullet theory. The *Hampshire Chronicle* said that it was fairly certain that Messiter had been shot from behind, and stressed the importance of finding the bullet. The matter was resolved when Sir Bernard Spilsbury, the famous pathologist, said that Messiter had probably been struck down with the hammer – there had been three massive blows to the head by some heavy implement. The hammer had traces of blood on its head and on its shaft, and on the wood protruding from the socket of the head were two hairs, which on examination under the microscope proved to be identical to the hairs in the dead man's eyebrows. The *Hampshire Chronicle* suggested that the crime was unpremeditated otherwise a more suitable weapon would have been used. (If this was the murder weapon it had proved remarkably effective.) A photograph of the hammer was printed in the local newspapers with a request for anyone who could identify it to contact the police.

Spilsbury said that it was almost certain that Messiter had been struck while in a stooping position, perhaps examining his oil cases, which were spattered with blood, the blow hitting him on the back of the neck, which would have shattered his skull. The second blow was to the side of the head while the skull was on the floor, and the third blow, which landed on one of his eyebrows when he was flat on his back, finally finished him off.

But there were no clues as yet to the identity of the murderer. On the seat of the car were two books and in one of them were carbon sheets with names and addresses (which later proved to be fictitious) and orders for oil. Some pages had been torn out of each book, but indentations by a pen or pencil were observed on the succeeding pages. One of these read: 'October 28, 1928. Received from the Wolf's Head Oil Co. commission on Cromer and Bartlett 5 galls. at 6d. 2/6. W.F.T.' Who was W.F.T.? That was partly solved by the finding in the garage of a scrap of paper with the words: 'Mr.W.F.Thomas. I shall be at Grove Street at 10 am but not at noon. V.Messiter.' But who was W.F.Thomas?

94

Another vital clue came to light when Messiter's apartment was searched. There the police found a letter dated 23 October 1928 signed by William F. Thomas, who gave his address as 5 Cranbury Avenue, Southampton. It read: 'Sir, Re your advt. of the present inst. Being in the Motor Trade, and having a good connection amongst farmers and garage proprietors, I am sure I can do you good service in the oil lines. I am constantly asked my opinions of such, and I am sure I can build up a good connection.' The advertisement referred to, in the *Southern Daily Echo*, read: 'Wanted, experienced MAN, with knowledge of local conditions, to sell lubricating oils, on commission.'

The police went to 5 Cranbury Avenue, a guest-house kept by a Mrs Horne, who said that a couple named Thomas had stayed with her from 20 October to 3 November the previous year. The forwarding address they had given proved to be fictitious. From her description the police were able to issue particulars of Thomas, which described him as being about thirty-two years old, 5 ft. 4 or 5 in. in height, of pale complexion, dark hair and with a scar on his temple. With him was a woman aged about thirty with golden hair and known as 'Lil'. They were rewarded by a message from a firm at Downton, Wiltshire, who had employed Thomas as a motor mechanic for several weeks, from 3 November to 23 December. He had left suddenly, the day after the wages for the firm's employees had disappeared.

There was another clue at Cranbury Avenue – a sheet of paper with the name 'Podmore' and an address in Manchester. Enquiries at that address revealed that a man named Podmore had been employed there until 17 October 1928. The police were now sure that Thomas was William Henry Podmore, whom they knew to have a record of petty crime. Podmore was traced to a hotel in London through his girl-friend Lily Hambleton or Hambledon at Stoke-on-Trent, who told them where to find him. He said that he was about to travel to Southampton to tell what he knew of Messiter. He admitted being in the garage on 30 October but said that there had been another man with Messiter. The two of them had gone away and that was the last time he saw Messiter. The rest of his statement agreed with what the police already knew – his selling of oil on commission and his job at Downton.

In his statement Podmore confessed to the committing of thefts in Manchester, for which he was wanted by the police. To cover his tracks he came to Southampton with Lily Hambleton and assumed the name Thomas. He started to answer advertisements for jobs, including the one with Messiter and the one at Downton. The day after his interview with Messiter he had an interview at Downton and agreed to start work there on 5 November as a motor mechanic at 50 shillings a week. Did that mean that he intended to work for Messiter for only one week? Did he tell Messiter that?

Podmore then described his movements on Tuesday 30 October. He had borrowed Messiter's car to drive to Downton to see whether he could start work there immediately. On his return he found the garage locked so he left the car in the outer yard, there being no sign of Messiter. He made repeated attempts that week to start work at Downton as soon as possible and finally it was agreed that he would start on Saturday 3 November. He worked at Downton until 23 December, when a number of wage packets went missing. After being questioned by the police he left in a hurry for London and then went to Birmingham, where he reverted to the name Podmore once again. When the news of the murder appeared in all the newspapers Podmore was working at a hotel near Coventry with Miss Hambleton. They left immediately without collecting their wages, she going to her home and Podmore to London, where he was located after the Stoke-on-Trent police had interviewed Lily Hambleton.

The inquest was held on 15 March and the coroner's jury returned an open verdict. The police did not have enough evidence to charge Podmore with murder – it was all circumstantial. He had, however, confessed to thefts in Manchester, for which he was sentenced to six months imprisonment. When he was released he was charged with the theft of the wage packets at Downton. He confessed to that and received a further six months in prison. On his release he was charged with the murder of Messiter, which he strenuously denied, saying that he might be a thief but he had never been guilty of violence.

The trial of William Henry Podmore was held at Winchester in the week beginning Monday 3 March 1930 with Lord Hewart, the Lord Chief Justice himself, presiding. The prosecuting counsel was Sir Thomas Inskip, who had been Attorney-General in the last Government until his defeat at the general election in 1929. He had been the prosecuting counsel in the Allaway trial in 1922. The defence counsel was Mr H. du Parcq, KC. Many reporters from the national newspapers were present as the case had aroused widespread interest. Applications for permission to attend were received from all over the country (from the sort of people who in days gone by would have attended public hangings?) but none was granted and the attendance was strictly limited. One exception was the Bishop of Winchester, whose motive in attending can only be surmised.

Podmore seemed quite confident, probably because the inquest jury had not incriminated him, and his plea of 'Not Guilty' was made in a clear voice. He kept his eyes fixed on the bench and ignored the people in court. The jury consisted entirely of men from various parts of Hampshire. An exhibit in court that aroused much interest was a model of the garage and forecourt at Grove Street made to a scale of $^1/_2$ in. to 1 ft. with miniature oil cans in their exact positions when the body was found. The other exhibit was the hammer used by the murderer, which no doubt was viewed with a certain morbid curiosity.

Monday to Thursday was taken up with the hearing of evidence. Further evidence was given by two prisoners who were with Podmore in Wandsworth prison; they claimed that Podmore had admitted his guilt to them. In his summing up at the end Lord Hewart said that not too much reliance should be placed on that sort of evidence. On Friday the prosecuting and defence counsels made their concluding speeches. Sir Thomas Inskip's took an hour and a half and at the end he urged that the inferences to be drawn from the evidence were strong, cogent and irresistible, pointing to Podmore as 'the man who committed the murder'. Mr du Parcq's speech lasted for four hours (but perhaps that included a lunch break). His case rested on Podmore's complete denial of the charge. The reason for his sudden changes of address and his false name was the attempt to hide from the police after the Manchester and Downton robberies. He said that there was no direct evidence to incriminate Podmore (that was indeed true). The hammer could not be traced to him, there were no bloodstains on his clothes and nothing of Messiter's was found in his possession. The evidence, he submitted, was therefore entirely circumstantial. As it was then 4.30 pm Lord Hewart said that he would give his summing up the next day, and added, 'In the meantime, gentlemen, I am sure you will keep your minds open.'

On the Saturday Lord Hewart began his summing up at 10.30 am and spoke without a break until 1.50 pm. At the very outset he reminded the jury that the guilt of the accused had to be established beyond a reasonable doubt. 'Not beyond a fantastic, whimsical or capricious doubt, but such a reasonable doubt as would govern a man's course of action in some private affair of his own.' Having put the minds of the members of the jury at rest on that point (or maybe not!) he went on to examine the evidence by tracing the circumstances of the crime, and weighed the various pieces of evidence that were thought to connect Podmore with the murder. During the whole three hours or so Podmore rarely took his eyes off the judge and he seemed to become increasingly ill at ease as the evidence against him mounted. He relaxed towards the end, however, when Lord Hewart told the jury that they must not convict the accused merely upon suspicion – they must be satisfied that he was the man who had committed the murder.

Lord Hewart laid great stress on one piece of evidence, or rather its absence – the missing pages from the books, which had obviously contained detailed records of Messiter's business transactions. If Podmore was the murderer then he would cover his tracks by removing all evidence of business dealings between himself and Messiter. In other words who else but Podmore could possibly have had any interest in tearing the pages out of the books? He therefore suggested that only Podmore would have removed such evidence. It does not seem to have occurred to Lord Hewart that a clever murderer would do just that in order to throw suspicion on to Podmore.

The missing pages, went on the judge, judging from the indentations on the remaining pages and the carbon sheets, had contained records of fictitious orders with names of firms and addresses not known in Southampton, but known in the neighbourhood of the accused's home. Was it not an astonishing coincidence that at the very same time two different persons were making representations to Messiter about firms that did not exist and to whom he might possibly pay commission? These entries on the carbon sheets were not just names and addresses but were copies of invoices that Messiter had written out. It was therefore important that the jury should decide whether or not they were satisfied that the initials on the receipt from the Cromer and Bartlett transaction were indeed the initials of the accused.

The judge warned the jury that if the effect of all the evidence was no more than to leave on their minds a strong suspicion then they would have to acquit the accused. But if the effect of the evidence as a whole was to leave no reasonable doubt in their minds that Podmore was the murderer then they must find him guilty. He reminded the jury that the evidence was circumstantial (as indeed the defence counsel had submitted) as distinct from direct evidence, that is the evidence of an eye-witness, who could be biased or mistaken. He gave his own definition of circumstantial evidence: 'That when you look at all the surrounding circumstances you find such a series of undesigned, unexpected coincidences that as a reasonable person you find that your judgement is compelled to one conclusion. If the circumstantial evidence is such as to fall short of that standard, if it does not satisfy that test, if it leaves gaps, then it is of no use at all.'

The jury were convinced by the arguments of Lord Hewart and Sir Thomas Inskip and after retiring for an hour and twenty minutes (which included time for lunch) returned to give their verdict of 'Guilty'. There was a gasp from the public in the court then dead silence as the judge put on the black cap to pronounce the death sentence. Podmore was asked whether he had anything to say. 'I have, sir. I repeat that I know nothing whatever about it.' Lord Hewart then pronounced sentence of death. Many people inside and outside the court rushed to Trafalgar Street to get a close look at the prisoner and jostled with a large number of press photographers. But they were all disappointed because a taxi was brought into Castle Square and Podmore was taken away almost unnoticed.

Podmore was executed at Winchester on 22 April 1930. Was he guilty? Probably – but who would stake any money on it? As Mr Justice Day remarked, at the James Parker murder trial in 1886, the fact that someone was the last person to have been seen or known to have been in the company of another person who was found murdered was not sufficient to prove his or her guilt. Did not that observation apply to Podmore? What was Podmore's motive in killing Messiter? Surely not for the small amount of money involved in the commission on oil sales. Why did Podmore, after killing Messiter and discovery possible at any minute, spend time in going through the invoice books when he could have stuffed them in his pocket? In fact if he had left them intact he might not have been found guilty of anything more serious than swindling, and if he had taken them away he could hardly have been convicted on the remaining evidence. These are questions that will never be answered but give rise to all sorts of intriguing speculations. The inquest jury decided there was not enough evidence. The trial jury considered the same evidence but decided there was enough evidence. Who was right?

MURDER ON THE TRAIN

O n Monday 29 June 1964 the 3.25 pm train from Southampton
to Reading had just left Basingstoke station after a brief stop
when a twelve-year-old schoolboy went to the toilet in the
front carriage of the three. Lying on the toilet floor was the body of
fifteen-year-old Yvonne Laker, with her throat cut and blood all over
the toilet compartment.

The boy told one of the men in the carriage who, after a brief look
at the dead girl, pulled the communication cord. When the train
stopped about 400 yards from the station the boy ran back down the
line to raise the alarm. After a few minutes the train reversed back to
the platform and the passengers changed to another Reading-bound
train, while the other train was put in a siding.

Yvonne Laker had boarded the train at Southampton after spend-
ing the weekend with her grandparents at Barton on Sea. Her parents were in Singapore, where her father was serving in the RAF. She
was returning to her convent boarding-school in Maidenhead.

That evening Detective Chief Superintendent Walter Jones of the
Hampshire CID arrived to investigate the tragedy, which from what he
had already been told sounded like a case of murder. When he got
there he was dumbfounded to discover that the local police had
removed the body to the mortuary and had ordered the railway staff
to clean the toilet compartment. In doing so they had removed every
scrap of evidence that might have given a clue to the killer's identity –
fingerprints, bloodstains, footprints and pieces of fibre from the girl's
clothes were all gone. The girl's body had not only been removed but
had been wrapped in a couple of old blankets, making examination of
her clothes now useless. The first principle of a murder investigation
is not to move the body. To make matters even worse, all the passengers who had alighted from the train after it reversed had been
allowed to disappear without any record of their names. In answer to
this catalogue of disaster the local police and railway staff could only
reply that they had no reason to suspect murder and thought it was
suicide. A girl lying dead with injuries she could hardly have inflicted
herself, and no implement in the toilet anyway that she could have
used, and they did not suspect foul play! To say that Jones was angry
would be the understatement of his career.

It was thought that the girl was killed between Micheldever and
Basingstoke, either in the carriage or after being taken to the toilet. At
the time there was probably no-one else in the carriage, which was of

the open type divided into sections with no corridor through to the other carriages. After a search of the railway track Yvonne's shoes and beret were found, together with some broken glass.

The killer must have left the train either at Basingstoke or when it slowed to a walking pace as it neared the station. An appeal to passengers on that train to contact the police resulted in 40 people who had used it on some part of its journey giving statements. The police particularly wanted to interview those passengers who had alighted from or boarded the train at Basingstoke, not all of whom had yet been found.

On the Tuesday of the following week the police interviewed twenty-seven-year-old Derek Pye, who was in custody at Aldershot police station on two charges. Pye was an unemployed farm-worker who lived at Long Sutton with his wife and three children. As a result of this interview the officers took him to Basingstoke police station, where he was charged with the murder of Yvonne Laker. When told he was to be charged Pye said, 'I never touched the girl. I had nothing at all to do with it. I would never bring shame to my wife and children.' Later he said, 'Damn good life my kids are going to have with no father.' The next day he appeared in court and was remanded in custody for a week. Crowds of women waited silently in the rain to see him brought to the court, and were rewarded by the sight of Pye with his head and shoulders covered in a blanket.

The case before the Basingstoke magistrates lasted for four days. It was Basingstoke's longest-ever murder hearing as 56 prosecution witnesses took over twenty-one hours to give evidence. Pye pleaded 'Not Guilty' and reserved his defence. Lewis McCreery, prosecuting counsel, outlined his case against Pye. He said that although several people had entered and left the carriage during the journey it appeared that Yvonne and her killer were the only occupants of the murder compartment after the train left Winchester. He pointed out that there was no corridor connection between the first-class and second-class sections. It is not clear what he meant by that (see further on). No-one from the front carriage had alighted at Micheldever, according to four passengers who alighted from the rear carriage there. Several people got into the carriage at Basingstoke, including a woman who said that she saw a young man get out and hurry away.

The fragments of glass found on the track and in the train had been pieced together, and the number on the base of the bottle and pieces of a label proved that they came from a half-bottle of Questa sherry. Several sherry bottles had been found at Pye's house, including a half-bottle of the same make. At first Pye denied buying a half-bottle of sherry that day, but later admitted buying one from the Grapes Hotel in the evening. Later still he denied having gone to the Grapes. The licensee of the Grapes said that a man bought a half-bottle of sherry at about 1 pm. McCreery suggested that that man was Pye. (But the licensee failed to pick Pye both at an identification parade and at the magistrates court, in spite of saying that he would remember him.)

Three days after the murder Pye had stolen a car and crashed it at Crondall. He had been arrested and detained at Aldershot police station. While there he said to a police officer, 'I am worried. I was on the train where the girl was murdered. I saw a man drag her along the corridor to the toilet.' He was sobbing as he said this. This was the first indication that Pye had been on that train. He then went on, 'That train murder. I think I know who did it.' Asked why he had not come out with this information before he replied, 'The newspapers said it happened on a crowded train. As there were only us three I didn't think it could be the same one.'

Pye had described his movements on that Monday. He had first gone to the employment exchange at Basingstoke, then was going to Winchfield (two stops on the London line) but got on the Reading train by mistake. He returned to Basingstoke then decided to go to the Royal Marines recruitment office at Winchester. After that he boarded the train at Winchester station and sat in a compartment containing the girl and another man. He went to the toilet and when he came out the man was helping the girl along towards it. Asked what was wrong the man said that the girl had been sick. He took her into the toilet and after two or three minutes came out alone. Pye asked him whether she was all right to which the man replied that it was none of his business. Pye went to the other end of the carriage, found some glass on the seat and threw it out of the window. He got off the train at Basingstoke and later caught another train to Hook, where he took a taxi to Odiham on his way home. (The taxi-driver on duty at Hook that evening said that he took no-one to Odiham.) Pye's next-door neighbour said that he spoke to him at home between 8.30 and 9 pm.

The ticket-collector at Basingstoke said that there was no man among the people who left the platform after the train pulled out. (But another witness said that a young man got off the train.) He said that a man had walked through the barrier twenty minutes later and put 2 shillings on the ledge. McCreery wondered whether that man was Pye, afraid to leave the station immediately, or perhaps he had been to the toilet to clean himself. (Surely the train would have reversed back by then and the police have arrived?) Pye in his evidence said he was the man in question. He said he had taken a train to Hook at 6 pm but he was seen on Basingstoke station at 7.30 pm by someone who knew him. A witness from the Wilts and Dorset bus station said that Pye entered the café there soon after the train left and bought a coffee. (He denied this.) His account of that day seems to have been a tissue of lies. McCreery said that his description of the events on the train was wholly false. (He meant unbelievable – not necessarily false.)

One of the witnesses called by the prosecution was Nigel Gulliver, a porter at Winchester station. He said that Pye had got into the first carriage and sat in the second-class section on the right-hand side facing Basingstoke. He saw a young girl sitting on the long (?) seat of that section or compartment. He thought there were other people in the carriage. (He must have been wrong – nobody from that carriage got out at Micheldever according to the four witnesses.) Throughout the hearing and the subsequent trial there seemed to be much confusion about the description of the train. It apparently did not have Pullman carriages but carriages of open plan with an aisle in the middle and no tables, and the first carriage at least was divided into first-class and second-class sections, or compartments as they were loosely called. Witnesses who referred to a corridor or passageway presumably meant an aisle or gangway down the middle of the carriage.

At the end of the hearing defence counsel Terence Read asked for the other serious offences for which Pye was in custody to be adjourned as the evidence in those cases might prejudice his defence on the murder charge. The chairman of the magistrates rejected Read's application. It was later decided, however, that evidence on those other charges would be heard in camera so as not to prejudice the murder charge.

Pye's trial began on Monday 23 November, when he pleaded 'Not Guilty'. Jeremy Hutchinson for the prosecution said that 'this dreadful murder' was all the more terrible because it occurred in broad daylight on a summer afternoon in June on an ordinary train journey between Winchester and Basingstoke. The girl had been struck with a bottle with sufficient force to break the bottle and her throat had then been cut with the broken end. There had been no sexual assault and no robbery – her purse and gold wrist-watch had not been taken. He said that her shoes and beret had been found on the track, thrown out by the killer, and pieces of the bottle had been found on the track, supposedly thrown out by Pye. Were there really two men throwing things out of the train, he asked? Was Pye telling the truth?

Dr Keith Simpson, the pathologist, took two hours to describe the girl's injuries and the conclusions he had drawn from them. (By which time the jury must have been a little restless.) He said that a wound over her left eye could well have been the result of a blow from a bottle of sufficient force to break the bottle. The cut across her throat looked as if it had been done with the broken end of the bottle; if the throat had been cut from behind her there would be no blood-stains on her attacker's clothes. David Croom-Johnson, defence counsel, asked that photographs of the dead girl be shown to the jurors. Mr Justice Streatfeild ordered the jury to examine the pictures 'in the pursuit of justice'. Dr Simpson said that dirt on the girl's knees and toes was consistent with her having been dragged along the corridor.

Croom-Johnson said there had been no evidence from the prosecution to prove that there was no other man on the train between Winchester and Basingstoke (he meant in the carriage). A witness said that a man was seen walking along the track in the opposite direction soon after the train passed as it neared Basingstoke. Some railway workers also saw a man walking towards them from the direction of Basingstoke. He was acting rather suspiciously and seemed in a hurry. After walking some distance towards Winchester he turned off the track. Another witness said that the train as it approached Basingstoke slowed down enough for a man to have jumped off safely. Croom-Johnson reminded the jury that no blood had been found on Pye's clothes, a remarkable fact in view of the girl's injuries. Pye had volunteered all the information he could in order to help the police, and then finished up by being charged with murder. He said, 'If this situation was not so serious it would be almost funny.'

When called to give evidence Pye could not say how the glass had got in his pocket, but he certainly had no bottle with him on the train. In answer to a question from Hutchinson, Pye said that there was no blood on the man when he came out of the toilet, nor was there any blood on the girl when she was being dragged along the corridor. (He may have been correct in this; the blow on the head may not have caused much bleeding, unlike the cut to the throat.) Pye was asked why he had at first denied buying a bottle of sherry and later admitted to having done so. He replied that he could not remember when he had bought it. Good news for Pye came from the analyst, Dr Grant, who said that the glass in Pye's pocket could not have come from the bottle used in the murder, nor were there any fibres from the girl's blazer on Pye's clothes.

Mr Justice Streatfeild began his summing up by warning the jury that they should not be swayed by emotion because of the horrible nature of the crime. They were there to see that justice was done by assessing the evidence that had been presented to the court. He was appalled by the thought that there was a man capable of 'such a foul deed'. The judge was of course speaking in 1964 when atrocities like this were perhaps not so common as they are now. He said there was no question of insanity, nor was manslaughter an alternative verdict. It had to be 'Guilty' or 'Not Guilty' on the murder charge. He pointed out that Pye had been interrogated seven or eight times, and that he had stuck to the details of his story from start to finish.

The judge said that this case had attracted a great deal of newspaper publicity all over the country. If a man breaks a bottle over a girl's head and then cuts her throat with it there is no question but that it is wilful murder. There is no possibility of the charge being reduced to manslaughter, on the grounds of either diminished responsibility or insanity. He told the jury that if they thought that Pye's explanation might be true, even although wrong in some details, then he could not be convicted. The jury must not think that a crime was going unpunished and that they had to find a culprit. All they had to decide was whether they were sure that Pye was the culprit.

When the jury retired at midday on Tuesday the trial was in its seventh day. What was the evidence in favour of Pye? 1. He had volunteered the information that he was on the train when he need not have done so. 2. There was no blood from the girl on his clothes, nor any fibres from her clothes. 3. The glass in his pocket was not from the murder weapon. 4.There was no motive. What was the evidence against him? 1. No-one else had seen the man that Pye supposedly saw on the train with the girl, unless he was the unidentified man on the track. (Pye could equally well have been the man on the track.) 2. The taxi-driver denied taking Pye to Odiham. 3. Why did Pye throw pieces of glass from the window – just as dangerous as leaving them on the seat? 4. Most people would have become suspicious at seeing a man dragging a girl into a toilet. Why did Pye not say anything to the station staff at Basingstoke? 5. Why did he at first deny buying a bottle of sherry? 6. A similar bottle was found at his house. 7. The killer would surely not have hit the girl knowing that Pye was somewhere in that carriage and might see him do it. 8. Where did the killer, if it was not Pye, get on the train? There was much conflicting evidence.

The jury deliberated for six and a half hours. When they returned the foreman announced the verdict as 'Not Guilty'. Pye was held in custody, however, until the next assizes in March 1965, when he was put on trial for two other offences. These offences were not made known to the jury, luckily for Pye. What did the jury talk about for six and a half hours? It was clear to the defending counsel that whether or not he had committed the murder there was not enough evidence to convict Pye. The prosecuting counsel probably thought so too, but of course could not say so. The judge hinted as much when he told the jury that if they had any doubts about the prosecution case it was their duty to return a verdict of 'Not Guilty'. But of course the reason that there was not enough evidence to convict whoever had committed the murder was that the police had destroyed it all when they cleaned the toilet and removed the body. After that act of sheer stupidity there was not much to go on.

At the trial in March 1965 Pye was found guilty of setting fire to a barn at East Woodhay, setting fire to furniture at a house in Basingstoke, breaking into that house and stealing a camera and a radio from it. He was found not guilty of setting fire to three other barns in the same area. He was said to have three previous convictions, two for larceny and one for assault causing bodily harm. He was then charged with assaulting Leonard Mills, wounding his own wife Irene, and driving away a car without the owner's permission. He pleaded 'Not guilty' to the assault charges and 'Guilty' to the offence relating to the car.

Jeremy Hutchinson, the prosecuting counsel, said there was conflicting evidence regarding the first assault charge. On the second charge he understood that Pye's wife would be a reluctant witness. In the circumstances, therefore, he was not going to offer any evidence on either assault charge. With regard to the car offence there was no question but that Pye had taken it and crashed it at Crondall. The defence counsel pleaded in mitigation that Pye had now been in custody for nearly nine months and had had to endure a murder trial lasting several days.

The jury retired for six hours before finding him guilty. He was sentenced to eighteen months in prison on all the charges except the car offence, to run concurrently, to commence from the previous September. For the car offence he was sentenced to one day's imprisonment. He got off comparatively lightly because the judge felt that he had suffered enough at the murder trial, and but for that would have been sentenced to four years in prison.

DEATH IN A TAXI

At about 7.30 am on Thursday 22 October 1964 a woman walking her dog along Hursley Road turned into the lane leading to Hawstead Farm, between Chandler's Ford and Hursley. A few yards down the lane she saw a man lying on the grass verge. She stopped to take a closer look and saw to her horror that the man was dead, with a wound and congealed blood on the side of his head. He was dressed in grey trousers and a sports jacket and appeared to be in his sixties. She hurried away to call the police and at 8 am Police Constable David Browning arrived at the scene. After inspecting the body he found a pair of broken spectacles and a cap not far away.

When more police arrived they cordoned off the area around the body and waited for Dr Keith Simpson, the Home Office pathologist, to examine the dead man. When he had done so the body was removed to Southampton. The dead man was named as George Newbery, a sixty-year-old Southampton taxi-driver of Northumberland Road, who had been reported missing. His taxi had been found parked on waste land at the junction of Derby Road and Cranbury Avenue, not far from his home. Meanwhile the police, with the help of dogs, made a thorough search of the adjoining woods and farmland. Not far from the body they found a piece of gas piping 19 inches long with traces of blood on one end, which may have been the weapon used in what had evidently been a murder.

The main task confronting Detective Chief Superintendent Walter Jones of the Hampshire CID was to trace the movements of Newbery's cab, and to that end he made an urgent appeal to any members of the public who may have seen the cab that evening to contact the police. Sixty detectives, working from Southampton police headquarters, were assigned to the case.

George Newbery had been a taxi-driver since the age of eighteen. He had been in business ever since he took over from his father as an owner-driver, with the exception of the war years when he served in Southampton Fire Service. His regular taxi-rank was at Queen's Terrace, opposite the main gate of the docks, and consequently many of his customers were seamen. That particular rank is quite dark and lonely at night. It was Newbery's habit to accept his last fare before 9.30 pm and then garage his taxi-cab near the Polygon and walk home, or if late park outside his house. He was by all accounts a quiet, unassuming man who would never argue with his customers. He never carried much money with him – just enough for petrol.

When he did not return home on the Wednesday evening his wife assumed at first that he had broken down or perhaps driven someone to London, which he did occasionally.

The police had to find the answers to three important questions. Firstly, who were the two men who hired Newbery's cab, a biscuit-coloured Ford Consul, at about 9.45 pm at Queen's Terrace? Secondly, did anyone see the cab that evening between Southampton docks and Chandler's Ford or Hursley? Thirdly, did anyone see the cab being parked on the waste land at Cranbury Avenue between 10 and 11 pm? Residents in that area were particularly requested to come forward with any information. Newbery never parked on that spot himself. Was it just a coincidence that the cab had been parked so near to Newbery's home? Was the murderer someone who lived nearby and knew him? Or was it just a convenient place to dump a car when someone was in a hurry to get back to the docks? What was the motive for the murder? Robbery? If so then the murderer was unlucky. Newbery had no known enemies.

It was discovered that two men had seen the dead body in the dark before the woman stopped to look at it. A man who lived at the end of that lane said that he saw something or somebody on the ground at about 11.30 pm when he returned home, and assumed it was a pile of rubbish or even a tramp asleep. A milkman who delivered milk to the cottages in that lane also saw the body at about 7 am. He thought it was a 'dummy or something'. He saw two feet sticking out and the side of a face but did not stop to investigate.

The police maintained an extensive search for any possible clues or leads to the murderer. They called at houses in Chandler's Ford, they spoke to motorists travelling along Hursley Road, and they broadcast an appeal at the Saturday football match between Southampton and Leyton Orient. As a result one man at least was able to provide an eye-witness acccount. A docker who knew Newbery saw his cab parked in West Quay Road at about 10.05 pm that Wednesday. In the back were two men looking in the direction of the quays. (Were they the two men who had hired the cab at 9.45 pm at Queen's Terrace?)

The police murder squad apparently considered the possibility of a revenge killing as the motive for the crime. A Maltese man wanted for murder had been arrested in the same road in which Newbery lived and it was said (quite wrongly) that Newbery was the informant. Each cab-driver in Southampton was asked to give full details of his cab passengers on the Wednesday evening and whether he thought any of them suspicious in any way.

The liner *Queen Mary* sailed from Southampton on the Thursday morning and police at its ports of call were asked to interview members of the crew (but apparently not passengers). When it arrived at New York the police made a search but said that they could not interview all 1094 members of the crew. (They could but they would not?) When the ship arrived back in Cherbourg detectives from Southampton went on board and issued questionnaires to the crew asking for information on their movements on the day of the murder. Many of them had taken taxi journeys that day but none in Newbery's cab.

After the police appeal for witnesses a taxi-driver said that he saw Newbery's cab at about 11 pm being driven along Bevois Valley Road towards Cranbury Avenue. This witness helped the police to build an identikit picture of the man driving it. The police had still not heard from the two men who hired the cab at Queen's Terrace, or indeed from anyone who had used that cab that evening, including the two men seen in the cab in West Quay Road and a young couple said to have been inside it between 10 and 10.20 pm. Of the owners of the 20 to 25 cars and lorries parked on the waste land only half a dozen had contacted the police. All laundries and dry-cleaners in Southampton were asked to keep a look-out for bloodstained clothes. An appeal to the 500 or so people who had taken taxi-rides in Southampton that evening to come forward with information brought just five replies!

Superintendent Jones was now working on the assumption that Newbery had been attacked in his cab on the way out of Southampton. At the inquest on the Monday following the murder it was revealed that Newbery had died of a fractured skull and contusion of the brain. The inquest was adjourned until 26 January.

The murder hunt switched to the high seas on the Tuesday, when the cargo ship *Benvorlick*, anchored in the Thames estuary, was boarded by detectives who interviewed members of the crew. The *Benvorlick* had set sail from Southampton at 3.10 am on the Thursday, a few hours after the murder, and had just returned from a voyage to Zeebrugge. Police forces at ports of arrival had been asked to check other ships that left Southampton that morning.

Southampton police asked parents whether their children had been given any old clothes (perhaps bloodstained) for a Guy Fawkes dummy. (They obviously thought very little of the murderer's intelligence.) But still they could not identify the two men who hired the cab at Queen's Terrace or the man seen driving the cab towards Cranbury Avenue. Sometime later a new witness appeared.

A motorist had stopped behind Newbery's cab at traffic-lights in London Road at about 10.05 pm and had noticed a man and a girl with long blonde hair in the back. The police now started looking for a girl with long blonde hair. (It was to prove a false trail.)

The police drew up the following timetable of the cab's movements: 9.45 pm Queen's Terrace – picked up two passengers; 10 pm Cumberland Terrace – man and woman passengers; 10.05 pm West Quay Road – two passengers; 10.05 pm London Road heading towards The Avenue – man and a blonde; 10.55 pm Bevois Valley Road – man driver; 11.15 pm body seen in the lane. Some of those times must have been incorrect because they overlap, or the identification was faulty. (There was one other taxi-cab of the same colour working in Southampton.)

The funeral of George Newbery took place on Friday 30 October at St Matthew's church. Most of Southampton's 170 taxi-drivers attended, causing a severe shortage of taxis in the city for two or three hours.

The police were faced with many puzzling questions and a shortage of witnesses. It would seem to have been a coincidence that the cab was finally parked so close to Newbery's home, because if the driver knew where he lived he would hardly have risked being seen by a neighbour, even at that late hour. Yet the driver seemed to know his way around that district, at least in so far as locating a piece of waste land. Why had none of the passengers seen in the cab come forward? One obvious reason was that they had all left the city the following day, on a ship or a train, and were quite ignorant of the murder hunt that was proceeding. Another reason was that two of them were in fact the murderers. A third reason was that they were all frightened to come forward because they had no alibi if they were suspected of the murder. Were there no fingerprints on the iron bar or the steering wheel of the cab?

At the height of the investigations 60 police officers were working full time on the case. They visited 3500 houses, interviewed more than 6000 people, took 1600 sets of fingerprints from residents and seamen, and scanned 100,000 documents. Such an intense and thorough police search had rarely been seen in Southampton. Yet at the end of it the enquiries seemed to have produced no result.

Mrs Newbery had said that her husband had his Post Office savings book with him that evening. It was not on him when he was found nor in the cab. Soon after the murder a check had been made on all withdrawals in the Southampton area from the date of the murder. Eight days later the Post Office notified Jones that £3 had been withdrawn in Newbery's name from Woolston post office on the day after the murder. The withdrawal form had been traced (luckily they had been kept) and it was tested for fingerprints at Southampton. Although several people had handled the form only one fingerprint was revealed, but it was a good impression. Unfortunately it did not tally with any print so far obtained from Southampton residents or from any person in the police records. Everyone who could possibly have handled the form was fingerprinted and was eliminated. But the print might yet prove invaluable. The police continued their interviewing and fingerprinting, hoping that eventually they would get a similar print.

It seemed to Jones now that in all probability the fingerprint on the withdrawal form was that of the murderer, but who was he? Short of fingerprinting the whole population of Great Britain there seemed no way of finding out. The handwriting on the withdrawal form was examined by experts and compared with tens of thousands of forms – driving licence applications, Labour Exchange forms and suchlike – but nothing came of that.

Then out of the blue came a breakthrough. Since the murder Jones had instructed the CID to take the fingerprints of everyone charged with even the most trivial offence. A young man had been caught trying to break into a garage and was duly fingerprinted and released on bail. In the course of a routine check someone spotted that one of his fingerprints matched the one on the withdrawal form. His name was John William Stoneley. He was traced to a house in Lymington and taken to the police station. Jones felt sure that he had got the right man but he had to be careful lest by asking the wrong questions he might let him slip out of the noose. Stoneley could after all say that he had found the bank book in the street and there would be no way to disprove that.

Jones asked him first whether he had ever made a withdrawal from Newbery's account. 'No,' replied Stoneley. Asked whether he had ever used a bank withdrawal form he again replied, 'No.' He denied any knowledge of Newbery or his bank book. If he had been intelligent enough to think quickly he would have said that he had found the book in the street. But he had already done two incredibly stupid things – making a withdrawal from the murdered man's account and breaking into a garage and having his fingerprints taken. Indeed but for the second of these errors it is fairly certain that he would never have been caught, for Jones certainly did not intend to fingerprint the entire population.

As a result of this painstaking piece of detective work John Stoneley, a twenty-one-year-old cable-maker, and George Sykes, a twenty-three-year-old dairyman, appeared at Romsey magistrates court on 12 February 1965 charged with the murder of George Newbery. When confronted with the evidence of the fingerprint both men had admitted that they were the men who had attacked Newbery.

Peter Barnes, for the Director of Public Prosecutions, outlined the details of the case and the contents of the written statements from the prisoners. Stoneley had struck the fatal blows, but Sykes knew from the start of the cab journey that the intention was to rob Newbery, but not to kill him. The victim had received seven blows to the head with a length of iron gas piping. Bloodstains in the cab indicated that he had been sitting in the driver's seat at the time, then dumped on the ground and left. He had died a few hours later. When Stoneley was first interviewed after the discovery of the bank withdrawal he denied all knowledge of it. Later he was questioned by Walter Jones and said, 'This is the end of the world for me. I was just beginning to settle down, when this happened. Please help me.' He was to have been married a few weeks after the murder but had cancelled the arrangement without giving a reason.

Stoneley then wrote a long statement for the police. In it he said that he and Sykes had left their lodgings that evening with the intention of stealing some money. They took the iron piping in order to break open a cigarette machine. Then they decided to go for a ride in a taxi and run off without paying. They found Newbery at Queen's Terrace and after going to West Quay Road to look for some girls they eventually drove to the Hawstead Farm lane. They were about to get out and run away when Newbery, sensing they were up to no good, sounded the horn and put his foot on the accelerator. This frightened Stoneley, who then smashed the piping on Newbery's head. They left him on the side of the lane and Stoneley drove the cab back to Southampton. On the way he suggested ringing the police in case Newbery was dying but Sykes told him not to say anything otherwise he would kill him. The statement concluded, 'I am not guilty of murder but only of grievous bodily harm.'

When Sykes was interviewed he said that they needed money to pay their rent. He said that Stoneley had suggested hitting a taxi-driver on the head but he (Sykes) would not agree to that. He said, 'I did not touch the driver at all. I did not hit him and we did not intend to kill him.'

Dr Simpson, the pathologist, was asked whether Newbery's death was caused by being left unattended after the attack. He said that it was unlikely that Newbery would have survived after such severe blows to the head, causing fracture of the skull and contusion of the brain. There were far more blows than were necessary merely to knock him unconscious. He said that death would have occurred at some time, but 'not too long', after the attack. Both men were committed for trial at Winchester assizes.

The trial began on Monday 5 April 1965, Mr Justice Barry presiding. David Croom-Johnson, the Crown prosecutor, said that Stoneley, because he struck the blows, was charged with capital murder (death penalty), and Sykes with non-capital murder (no death penalty). Both men pleaded 'Not Guilty'. Most of his evidence was a repetition of that given at the Romsey magistrates court. When Cyril Harvey, Stoneley's defence counsel, opened his case he caused a surprise by stating that his client would not give evidence

Detective Inspector Rowe said that when he and Walter Jones interviwed Stoneley at Lymington about the savings bank withdrawal he denied having been to any post office in Southampton. Rowe read out the whole of Stoneley's written statement. Part of it read, 'I did not kill Mr Newbery... his death was caused by him not getting help. I wanted him to have it but Sykes would not let me. I only wish I had had the guts to go against Sykes.' Rowe said that Sykes had been convicted three times for stealing and once for housebreaking.

Lewis McCreery, Sykes's counsel, called him to the witness box and asked him, 'Do you accept responsibility for your part in the killing of George Newbery?' Sykes said that he did. 'If Stoneley had pleaded "Guilty" to that offence, what would your plea have been?' 'Guilty, sir.' ' Why are you pleading "Not Guilty" now?' 'Because I do not accept the things that Stoneley says in his statement,' replied Sykes. In his evidence he said that they read about Newbery's death in a newspaper, which came as a shock. Stoneley had said, 'The police don't know anything.' He told Stoneley they should clear out but Stoneley said the police knew nothing. (He was right – they knew nothing at that stage.) Sykes admitted that he had lied to the police on both occasions that he had been questioned.

Mr Justice Barry in his summing up told the jury that they had to be satisfied that Stoneley in fact killed Newbery and that he intended to kill him or cause serious injury. There could never be direct evidence of a man's intention but it had to be judged by the circumstances of the case. Capital murder could be committed only by a man who actually struck the blows while killing his victim in the course of theft. He told the jury that if they thought the blows were struck in panic and without spite and without intending to do grievous injury it was open to them to bring in a verdict of manslaughter.

The jury retired for only half an hour before returning a verdict of 'Guilty' on both men. The judge sentenced Stoneley to 'suffer death in the manner authorised by the law' and Sykes to life imprisonment. Neither of them showed any sign of emotion at the sentences. So ended a murder investigation that at one point looked as though it had reached no conclusion. If Stoneley had not been so stupid as to use the Post Office savings book there seems little doubt that they would have got away with the murder. It needs only one small and trivial piece of evidence to incriminate criminals who have made just one false move. The death penalty was abolished in 1965 so Stoneley was one of the first persons to benefit from the change in the law.

In a free vote on 21 December 1964 the House of Commons by 355 votes to 170 approved the abolition of the death penalty for murder for a trial period of five years. On 9 November 1965 the bill finally became law, and on 18 December 1969 the temporary law became permanent. Judge Barry had sentenced Stoneley to death because the measure had not then become law. The restoration of the death penalty has been debated a few times in Parliament since 1969. Hanging is still the punishment for treason and piracy. The last executions in Great Britain took place on 13 August 1964 when two men found guilty of murder were executed by hanging, one at Strangeways and one at Walton. No-one knew that they were to be the last executions in this country.

EPILOGUE

In ten of the murder cases in this book the verdict of 'Guilty' was a foregone conclusion. In the two Grayshott murders, however, the murderers were declared insane, one at the trial and the other one later by the Home Secretary. With hindsight it could be said that if Chapman and Codere were insane then so also surely was Frederick Baker. What of the other six cases? The verdict on Toplis, if he had lived, would certainly have been 'Guilty'. The murderer of Mary Pelham was never found. The Wield accident was a strange case. It should have been obvious that there was not enough evidence to incriminate Mrs Messenger and her son, but was it really an accident? In the trial of Burden the first jury failed to agree. The second jury, with the same evidence, soon came to a decision. The Podmore and Pye trials were in some respects similar. The evidence, as in the James Parker trial, was circumstantial, but whereas in that case Brown admitted his guilt, the other two protested their innocence. The jury took a long time to reach a decision in the Pye trial, and it would seem that both cases could have gone either way. In the end Pye was cleared, rightly because such evidence as remained was inconclusive, but Podmore unluckily was up against the Lord Chief Justice and the ex-Attorney-General and was convicted. It has to be said that the evidence against him was no stronger than against Pye, so he should have had the benefit of the doubt.

Fingerprinting was available to the police from 1901 and the first conviction as a result of it was in 1902. Yet the gun in the Wield case apparently was not tested for fingerprints, nor was the hammer in the Podmore case. Why not? Police detection excelled in the James Parker murder case, where but for Superintendent Sillence's intuition and skill the murderer would probably not have been found, in the Southampton taxi murder with the discovery of the fingerprint on the withdrawal form, and in the Podmore case although here it may have led to the wrong man. The rest were fairly routine investigations where it soon became clear who the murderer was. In the Wield case it seems that the police were too keen to put someone on trial and dropped any further investigations.

Of these 16 murders and one accident, three were committed with a gun, two with a razor, two with a broken bottle, one each with a hammer, knife, iron pipe, woodworking tool, lead stick, dagger, billhook and bayonet, and two (Galley and Chater) by brute violence. The motives in these murders were as varied as the means employed

115

in doing them. Theft accounted for five, rage or hatred for three and fear of the law for two (Galley and Chater). One was an accident, one was political or revenge (Buckingham), one was committed on impulse (Newbery) and four had no apparent motive (Yvonne Laker, Fanny Adams, Pelham and Huntingford). Three murders were committed by a husband on his wife or mistress, one by a wife on her husband. The others were committed on comparative or complete strangers.

In how many of the trials in this book was the accused wrongly convicted? Only three at the most (Huntingford, Burden and Podmore) but in the first two of them the evidence was fairly damning. A mistaken conviction before 1965 would have brought the death sentence, as with Timothy Evans and Hanratty. Whatever our views on the value of capital punishment as a deterrent to murder, the list of innocent people wrongly convicted by gullible juries and biased judges as a result of listening to persuasive counsels should be sufficient reason for its abolition.

BIBLIOGRAPHY

Anon (A Gentleman at Chichester), *The Genuine History of the Inhuman and Unparalell'd (sic) Murders Committed on the Bodies of Mr William Galley and Mr Daniel Chater* (1749)
Barnett, Correlli, *Britain and her Army* (1970)
Botley and Curdridge Local History Society Newsletter (1988)
Hampshire Chronicle
Jones, Walter, *My Own Case* (1966)
Lockyer, Roger, *Buckingham* (1969)
Nicholls, F.F., *Honest Thieves* (1973)
Portsmouth Evening News
Southern Evening Echo